NeWest
PRESS

Herbert
Has Lots For A Buck

How 12 Small Prairie Towns
Reinvented Themselves
For The 21st Century

Elizabeth
McLachlan

NeWest
Press

Copyright © Elizabeth McLachlan 2012

— — —

Library and Archives Canada Cataloguing in Publication

McLachlan, Elizabeth, 1957–
      Herbert Has Lots For A Buck: How 12 Small Prairie Towns Reinvented
      Themselves For The 21st Century/ Elizabeth McLachlan

Also issued in electronic format.
ISBN 978-1-927063-23-1
      1. Cities and towns--Prairie Provinces--Growth--History--
      21st century. 2. Prairie Provinces--Economic conditions--1991-.
      I. Title.

HT384.C32P73 2012   307.1'416309712   C2012-902347-7

— — —

Editor for the Board: Don Kerr
Cover and Interior Design: Greg Vickers
Author Photo: James Baron, Baron PhotoGraphics

Canada Council for the Arts / Conseil des Arts du Canada   Canadian Heritage / Patrimoine canadien   Government of Alberta   accessCOPYRIGHT FOUNDATION   arts council

NeWest Press acknowledges the financial support of the Alberta Multimedia Development Fund and the Edmonton Arts Council for our publishing program. We further acknowledge the financial support of the Government of Canada through the Canada Book Fund (CBF) for our publishing activities. We acknowledge the support of the Canada Council for the Arts which last year invested $24.3 million in writing and publishing throughout Canada.

201, 8540–109 Street
Edmonton, Alberta | T6G 1E6
780.432.9427
www.newestpress.com

NeWest Press

We are committed to protecting the environment and to the responsible use of natural resources. This book was printed on 100% post-consumer recycled paper.

1 2 3 4 5 13 12 | Printed and bound in Canada

Dedicated to **Connie Penner**

"Small towns more than 90 minutes drive from a city are usually locked in a struggle to avoid shrinking or dying. Just to maintain the size of a small town requires incredible ingenuity on the part of its citizens, or incredible desperation."

Fred Stenson
Alberta Views (July/August 2004)

"Herbert Has Lots For A Buck."

Promotional Sign
Outside Herbert, Saskatchewan

Table Of Contents

TABLE NO.	PERSONS	SERVER NO.	CHECK NO.	
			2571 - 5	

BEV • APPET • SOUP/SALAD • ENTREE • VEG • DESSERT

Thank You — Call Again

PERSONS	DATE	CHECK NO.	AMOUNT
		2571 - 5	

Prologue

Prologue

I recently drove through the tiny hamlet of Kirkcaldy, in southern Alberta. The town appeared to consist of one street that bowed off Highway 23 at one end and back onto it at the other. I thought it was deserted. There were abandoned buildings and ancient gas pumps, faded paint and broken windows. It was a bright midsummer's day, yet I saw not a soul.

But wait! There came a German shepherd, bounding happily out to greet me from a flower-gilded yard that was neatly grassed, trimmed, and (thankfully) fenced. And a little farther up the street stood a signpost, proudly announcing the Goldhawks lived here. Another residence, in an arty show of nostalgia, displayed a vintage Alberta Wheat Pool sign at the entrance to its well-kept driveway. Little Kirkcaldy was breathing. Her residents were affluent enough and cared enough to take pride in their yards and homes, to appreciate art and history.

But where was the church? The store? The school? The post office?

Throughout the Canadian prairies (as throughout Canada and the world) rural depopulation is a reality. The myriad reasons spin together in concurrent cause-and-effect cycles. To begin with, mechanization allows fewer people to accomplish more work. Family farms, once prolific enough to warrant a small school every four to six miles, grew in size and diminished in number; diesel locomotives eliminated the need for rural roundhouses and rail crews; dial telephones rendered exchanges obsolete; paved roads and better cars made travelling—and spending money elsewhere— attractive; straightened highways bypassed towns they once bisected; city department stores (and, later, big box chains) offered merchandise at prices small-town shopkeepers couldn't compete with; branch rail lines terminated passenger service, then freight service, and finally closed completely; grain companies decommissioned hundreds of community elevators; churches closed, government services withdrew, and school districts consolidated. Rural children bused to larger centres for their education never fully returned, their emotional ties with their home communities now weakened, and ease of travel and better job prospects luring them away. In a slow erosion, which began decades ago, farm kids, telephone operators, business owners, elevator agents, railway employees, teachers, post office workers, clergy—and anyone associated with failing businesses and discontinued services—headed for the cities, taking their families, tax dollars and civic leadership skills with them. They left landscapes strewn with abandoned buildings and thinning, aging populations. Cities growing fat with rural migrants soaked up the towns around them, encroaching on an ever-sparser countryside. In the 1940s, when the accumulation of all these changes finally tipped the scales, almost half of Canada's population was rural. Today, 80 per cent live in urban environments, and more than half the farms are large-scale, corporate, factory operations. Communities that once sustained, and were sustained by, agricultural surroundings, are dying. Add those struck down by resource depletion and the impact of climate change, and the course is set.

The economic, social, and environmental consequences of rural out-migration are well-studied and documented. The researchers I encountered—Drs. Dave Whitson and Debra Davidson (University of Alberta), Dr. JoAnn Jaffe (University of Regina), and Dr. Roger Epp (Augustana Campus, U of A)—are just a few who have made significant contributions to an understanding of rural degeneration. Their work represents a growing body of academic investigation into a field of escalating concern.

This book, however, is neither academic in nature, nor is it about degeneration. Rather, it is a look at communities that should have died, but didn't. Despite losing grain elevators, post offices, schools, grocery stores, and other essential services, they are thriving.

As I researched communities in Alberta, Saskatchewan

and Manitoba that found ways—often highly original ones—to attract new people, retain those who stayed, and stabilize economies, three varieties emerged:

(1) Towns that had died, or were dying, and came back to life.

(2) Towns which were still viable but sensed advancing deterioration.

(3) Towns that have been long dead, but have refused to go away.

The latter category includes places like Snipe Lake, Saskatchewan; Retlaw, Alberta; and Rowley, Alberta. In Snipe Lake, a single resident continues to live in and promote the town. She calls herself the mayor and, since she uses the town fire truck to water her garden, she lays claim to the title of fire chief as well. In Retlaw, a lone family dwells in a holiday trailer during mild months. Presumably they are the ones who every year plant flowerbeds, fill tubs, pots, and pails with abundant blooms, and watch over what's left of the community: a restored, historic church; a community hall; a ball diamond with "Retlaw's Field of Dreams" painted on its backstop, and a prettily appointed picnic shelter with the following posted message:

Retlaw Cook Kitchen There ain't no place just like this place anywhere near this place so this must be the place

A single door standing upright and alone on the prairie where houses and streets used to be is a surreal symbol of hope for future redevelopment. And in Rowley, affectionately referred to as Rowleywood, volunteers and summer students run tours of streets and buildings used as sets for a variety of commercials and movies—among them *Bye Bye Blues*, *The Pelican Brief*, *Unforgiven*, and *Legends of the Fall*.

Snipe Lake, Retlaw, and Rowley are just three of the many "dead" towns that continue to live in their own unique ways across the prairies. This book's primary focus, however, is on the other two categories of communities: those that died and came back to life, and those that foresaw their eventual demise and took steps to prevent it. They did this by focusing on one or more of six themes:

(1) Education

(2) History

(3) Culture

(4) Economic Development (new industry, tourism)

(5) Recreation

(6) Reinvention

Like the cause-and-effect spiral that brought rural communities down in the first place, these themes inseparably intertwine to build them back up. Often the lines between them are blurred. Craik, Saskatchewan, for example, hoped to attract new population and industry through reinvention as an ecologically friendly, self-sustaining community. Doing so, however, allowed it to tap into opportunities in **tourism**, **education**, **recreation**, and **culture** as well. Inglis, Manitoba wanted to both make and preserve **history** by restoring an entire elevator row, but the finished project is also an outlet for **education**, **culture**, and **economic development**. One theme naturally leads to another and residents simply take advantage of the doors that open to them.

I believed my greatest challenge when I began research would be tracking down enough death-defying towns for a whole book. I couldn't have been more wrong. My greatest difficulty was deciding which of dozens of success stories to leave out. Just a few years ago, towns that beat the survival odds were a phenomenon. Rebranding had yet to become the buzzword it is today. Now it is a trend. It seems every week another community makes headlines, doing something crazy, creative, clever, unexpected, desperate, risky, or any combination of the above, to keep from blowing away in the prairie dust. Torrington, Crowsnest Pass, Vauxhall, Nobleford, Eastend, Big River, Herbert, Waldheim, Gimli, Russell, Minnedosa... the list goes on. I can't possibly include all the towns I heard about, researched and sometimes visited. It is my hope that the four from each prairie province I did include reflect the experiences of many. Perhaps within these pages you will detect a certain spirit, imaginative concept or sense of place that resonates. Perhaps, if there is a need, the town within which your heart resides will find that spirit too.

A note on terminology: In Alberta, Kirkcaldy is considered a hamlet—an unincorporated community of at least five dwellings. In Saskatchewan, on the other hand, a hamlet need only have a commonly accepted name and boundary. To apply for village status in both provinces, hamlets must reach a minimum population of 300, but Saskatchewan communities need only 500 residents to graduate to town status and 5,000 to become cities, whereas

Alberta requires 1,000 and 10,000 residents respectively. Manitoba's municipal act distinguishes between rural and urban municipalities according to the number of residents per square kilometre. To avoid confusion, and to reinforce how the plight of rural depopulation affects communities of every size across all prairie provinces, I've chosen to use the term "town" generically. As well, I refer to towns, villages and hamlets, without distinction, as "communities."

Chapter 1
Herschel

Herschel

Ancient Echoes:
The Death and Rebirth of a Prairie Town

Nestled amidst the coulees forty kilometres west of Rosetown, Saskatchewan lies the sleepy village of Herschel. It's just a sprinkling of dwellings scattered haphazardly across the floor of the Eagle Creek valley. There are so many gaps where businesses used to be that the wide main street looks like the toothless grin of an old crone. Most of the buildings still standing are empty, their paint peeling or gone, their windows veiled with decades of grime. Prairie grass has crept through and taken over wherever it can catch hold. At the north end of the street a smattering of half-ton trucks park at irregular angles near the tavern door of a small, plain hotel. Its six rooms are seldom occupied.

There are 30 people living in Herschel, with a further 300 in the surrounding Rural Municipality of Mountain View, but you wouldn't know it. All that can be heard as you stand in the street are grasshoppers, gophers, and wind in the dry prairie grass.

Occasionally, though, a car or a farm truck rumbles past the cemetery and over the wooden bridge into town, negotiates the curve past the hotel and the two remaining grain elevators (now inland gathering points) and stops in the middle of Main Street. Literally, in the middle of the road. Its occupant jumps out and strolls into the post office. Debbie Rea is there, dispensing mail and conversation while performing her dual role as postmistress and village administrator. When her two children were small, Debbie's family occupied the living quarters in the back of the post office. Debbie left the door between the kitchen and mailroom open so she could watch the children while she stamped and sorted mail. But when the plumbing declined, and the slope in the floor increased, the post office relocated to the vacant Credit Union next door (formerly the Chinese restaurant), and Debbie and her husband bought the United Church manse, no longer in use since the church discontinued regular services. The manse is a 1950s bungalow with a full basement—one of the newest and nicest houses in Herschel. At eleven thousand dollars, it was also one of the most expensive.

Herschel wasn't always the semi-ghost town it appears today. When it was incorporated in 1911 it held great promise as a thriving agricultural and coalmining community. The future was so bright that the Methodist church's provincial Home Mission superintendent requested Herschel be sent its first permanent minister, eliminating the need for sporadic, itinerant services held in Cruickshank's General Store. Mr. W.J. Johnston was not ordained when he arrived from Ireland—he was only a candidate for the ministry—but he took his duties seriously, and in the small wooden building erected for the purpose he tended his meager flock with diligence. On July 4, 1911, when the first train arrived, Mr. Johnston was on hand to meet it. In due course he welcomed the first doctor, the first banker, and many others to the town, which eventually swelled to a population of approximately 300.

Perhaps it was this early spirit of community-mindedness that set the tone for what was to come. In 1925, when overcrowding demanded a new church building, support was so generous the collection plate at the inaugural service overflowed. The seven hundred and eighty-five dollars gathered was enough to lift the new church out of debt—news that inspired the entire congregation to rise in spontaneous song. When a larger building was again required forty years later, it was built entirely on volunteer labour, with only one carpenter hired as overseer. This church too was consecrated debt-free, even though by then the coalmine had long been closed. More than Methodists attended the opening service; other community members showed up as well, including Mennonites, whose local church choir graced the gathering with special music.

In 1957 an arena was built on the hill at the south end of town. Again, with the exception of a professional roofer, volunteers performed all the labour. When its fragile skeleton blew down in a storm, no one lost heart. A new framework was quickly raised and construction continued. By now the village had a school, hardware store, lumber yard, gas station, farm implement dealership, grocery store, and all the amenities of a farming community.

The ravine and acres of rolling prairie surrounding Herschel were a child's wonderland. Scores of youngsters allowed their imaginations to run free among the coulees. There was little danger. Plains grizzly bears that had once roamed freely hadn't been sighted since the 1920s, and no one had ever seen a rattlesnake. A short hike west of Main Street took the children to the town's water well, where they were enthralled by the little spring that bubbled up with water so gassy they could light it with a match. From there they headed to Eagle Creek to catch frogs. One special spot was named Frog Town for the hundreds of frogs that sang there. Then it was off to play cowboys and Indians at Indian Town—a series of three mounds the children imagined were Native burial grounds. There were large, strangely shaped rock formations there too. One of them looked just like an ancient oven.

In the winter the outdoor skating rink was busy. The girls skated and the boys played hockey. Curling was a favourite activity for all ages, especially once the new arena was established on the hill. Families joined together for socials in the community hall and visited daily with neighbours.

Construction of a new school, also on the hill, took place in 1961 and 1962. When it was finished, the boys of the community learned to mix and pour cement while working alongside their fathers to build a teacherage.

But as the children grew and gained greater access to the world around them thanks to better roads and the introduction of television, Herschel's identity as an entity unto itself wavered. High school students were bused to Rosetown where more educational opportunities were available. Eventually junior high students followed. When they graduated they moved away. Suddenly, not only were there no sons or daughters to take over family enterprises, but bigger businesses in larger towns lured consumers away as well. Herschel began to deteriorate as area population thinned, businesses dwindled, and grain elevators closed. Farm families no longer had reason to come to town, and those shops that remained slowly succumbed to the losing battle to stay open. In 1986, Herschel's last remaining grocery store burned to the ground. In time the bank and the bulk fuel dealership closed too. Families who'd lived in the community for years began trickling away. Herschel was breathing its last. Out at Indian Town, children no longer laughed and played. Only the occasional cow, horse, or hiker wandered by. The earth had gone silent.

Then, in 1990, near those three mounds, someone found a strange bone lying on the ground. It was too large to be human, but it was unlike any animal bone ever seen. Within days Herschel was crawling with archaeologists and paleontologists. First a perfectly preserved plesiosaurus was unearthed. The ancient reptile was estimated to be 65 million years old. Then another was found. And then a third; too fragile for excavation, however, it was covered back up. Virtually overnight Herschel was back on the map. For months crews came and went and the community enjoyed a brief burst of international acclaim.

The core of people still living in Herschel was small but dauntless, and they knew an opportunity when they saw one. The dinosaur discovery got them thinking about the area's history. Five thousand years ago, Blackfoot families had followed herds of bison across the land. They'd left plenty of evidence, but for years everyone had taken the tipi rings, arrowheads, and hammer heads for granted. In 1965, huge machines had scraped away an ancient medicine wheel to make room for a television tower. Two years later, elaborately carved rocks in a nearby pasture were finally reported as noteworthy, but it took eleven more years for the Saskatchewan Archaeological Society to investigate, and the fifteen-hundred-year-old petroglyphs weren't recognized as sites worth preserving for ten years after that.

When the dinosaurs were discovered in 1990, the whole town took an interest. Many turned out to work with the experts. Soon they were finding fascinating Blackfoot artifacts and beautifully preserved fossils dating up to five million years old. New energy and optimism infused the population, such that even the news of the final school closure didn't defeat them. The morning after the school division's fatal decision, Herschel's village council met and passed a resolution to request transfer of all school property to the town—for one dollar. Within six months they held title, and the Herschel Development Committee was soliciting funds and volunteers to renovate the building into the Ancient Echoes Interpretive Centre.

What transpired is amazing. In keeping with Herschel's history of community involvement, all the renovations were completed on volunteer time and labour. Volunteers organized tours to the excavation sites, stone effigies, tipi rings, and petroglyphs, all with the blessings of the farmers who owned the land. They created exhibits in the centre to showcase natural rock groupings, wood carvings, fossils, and ancient rock tools. Individuals combed their pastures and yards for more artifacts, many of which were simply lying on the ground. With the help of a local medicine man, who provided explanations of their uses for healing and nutrition, a collection of native plant species was added. New donations and displays continue to appear, and the centre is developing an impressive library of books, journals, and periodicals.

Volunteers do the paperwork to apply for grants and make sure the school-cum-interpretive centre meets the strict criteria of the Museums Association of Saskatchewan. The wall between the old home economics room and adjoining classroom was knocked out, allowing space for a pretty gift shop and tea room, also run by volunteers who bring homemade squares and cookies from their kitchens and bake dozens of Saskatoon berry pies. The facility is also a perfect venue to rent for special events both solemn and celebratory.

In 1996, a stunning new archaeological discovery was made: a two thousand-year-old buffalo jump, complete with slaughtering site, firepits, and more First Nation artifacts. About the same time, the Ancient Echoes Interpretive

Centre caught the attention of Métis artist Jo Cooper. As a result of a personal vision quest, she had recently completed a series of twenty paintings depicting the rise and fall of the buffalo, along with the people who depended upon them for survival. She was showing her art in Winnipeg when she heard about Herschel and felt compelled to move her work there. David Neufeld, head of the Herschel Development Committee, thought the prestigious artist had made a mistake when she called him to inquire about the possibility. He suggested more prominent galleries in Saskatoon or Regina, but Jo was insistent. Even though the village is so tiny that she drove straight through it, missing it entirely when she first arrived, she was undeterred. She and her exhibit were enthusiastically received, and the Ancient Echoes Interpretive Centre now boasts a bona fide art gallery in what used to be the school gymnasium.

Jo Cooper remained in Herschel for four months as artist-in-residence. Her exhibit fit the theme of the centre so perfectly that as time drew near for it to move on, Herschel decided they couldn't let it go. It would take twenty thousand dollars to purchase the collection, but area residents were indomitable. They came up with the money by hauling a decommissioned grain elevator into a field, painstakingly dismantling it and selling the prized wood, board by board. They didn't stop there. They encouraged Jo, who is also a photographer, to author a book about the collection, complete with images of the paintings. The interpretive centre published the book, titled *The Disappearance and Resurgence of the Buffalo*, in 2002, adding a further innovative source of income to their cause. The launch took place at McNally Robinson Booksellers in Saskatoon.

As it turned out, Herschel didn't just get the artwork; they got the artist. Jo was so taken with the community that she made it her second home.

The presence of the interpretive centre has sparked other ventures as well. Bed and breakfasts have opened, and so have a day spa and a retreat centre. Visitors can pay to spend the night in a tipi, part of the tipi village that has been erected in the town and from which a culture and survival camp is run. The Wiebe Berry Farm and Eagle Creek Outfitters have successful businesses. Others have also been drawn to Herschel. The centre has unused classroom space which can be rented at reasonable rates. Within a few short years a clothing factory moved in.

While the interpretive centre's hours are only part-time, it stays open year-round on the strength of volunteers. School tours are popular, and busloads of seniors come from surrounding communities to visit the tea room. A coordinator, hired on a part-time basis, plans May-to-September programming for all ages and oversees three summer students.

The friendly nature of Herschelites is legendary. Just ask Johanna Naubert and Rhonda Girling, partners in the Herschel Hotel. Johanna grew up on a farm and Rhonda has lived all over Canada. Both women swore they would never live in a small town again, but when the hotel came up for sale they decided to risk it. It's not a highly profitable venture, but it's something much better: it's friendship and community and belonging. Now the two women sing Herschel's praises as both a wonderful place to raise children and a great place to retire. Not surprisingly, their primary income is from the tavern, where those randomly parked trucks are often seen. Rhonda and Johanna keep the coffee pot hot for farmers who drop by throughout the day to help themselves. They chat with Johanna while she sits with needlework and play with Rhonda's son's cat. Before they leave they toss a loonie into the cup beside the pot. Occasionally someone will phone half an hour ahead for sandwiches or soup, at which point the two women take inventory of the larder and quickly whip up a tasty lunch based on what they find. One of many examples of their kindness took place when a camper in the nearby campground came in one day and asked to rent a room just so she and her daughter could shower. Johanna and Rhonda told them to go ahead, never mind payment. They even provided towels. They were surprised when they later discovered twenty dollars left for them on the dresser.

David Neufeld is not just the head of the Herschel Development Committee. He is also the mayor, and pastor of the Mennonite Church situated several miles out of town. He has a keen appreciation for the area's people and culture, both historical and contemporary, and his generosity is such that he is willing to meet the religious needs of anyone, Mennonite or not, in a village that has lost the services of all its other churches.

Clearly, despite its fervour and friendliness, Herschel still faces challenges. In 2005 village administrator Debbie Rea stated that since the two remaining elevators had been converted to farm storage they'd be assessed at a lower rate. "They're not worth as much," she said. "In fact, the town overall is not worth as much.... This year I lost several post office customers. Some moved away and some passed away." Yet the same year, "approximately fifteen thousand dollars was raised from the community for a memorial park playground and landscaping. Thirty thousand was raised for tin on the rink roof. This is ten thousand more than the original rink cost. Imagine what these projects would cost if not done voluntarily."

In 2010 the elevators are all gone, Debbie's children have grown, and the family has moved away. But the post office is still open, managed by another mother, who with her husband is raising children in the same area and tradition as her parents and grandparents. Lower village taxes and cheap real estate may draw more population and business to the community. And the interpretive centre is flourishing. "The paleontologists found a new species of plesiosaur," says Debbie. "It is to be named Herschelensis."

The passionate words of the late Elsie Mills, a longtime Herschel resident, reflect the sentiments of all Herschelites: "There is no question that the Ancient Echoes Interpretive Centre has kept Herschel alive."

It's true that if you stand in the middle of Main Street you will see and hear little more than the insects, gophers, and wind in the prairie grass. But from Main Street you can't see the school on the hill. That's where the action is, either in the tea room, the art gallery, the museum—or out on the prairie with the ancients.

Chapter 2
Rosebud

Rosebud

Commedia and Tragedy

Alma Siemens remembers the horror of the day it began. She wasn't there, but her friend LaVerne's anguish as he related the tragedy was palpable.

In 1973 LaVerne Erickson was a young man teaching in Calgary and engaged as a youth pastor. On a quiet Sunday afternoon he and some friends gathered for a Bible study at the home of an equally young junior high school teacher. After everyone had assembled, there came a knock on the door. The host was surprised and pleased to find several of her students standing on the threshold.

"They stuck their heads in and said hello," says Alma, "which was very unusual."

Obviously the teenagers liked their teacher well enough to drop in on her. Likely they were bored, but she was sensitive to their overture of friendship and quickly invited them in.

"Then they noticed all the 'older' young people in the room," says Alma, and declined the invitation.

The teacher and her friends protested. "Why do you have to go?"

"Oh... we have stuff to do."

"What do you have to do?"

"Nothing."

"Standard answer for young people," Alma says with a smile. But how bitterly LaVerne and his friends later regretted not pressing the matter.

"The next day they discovered that the 'nothing' these kids were doing was indulging in homemade brew," says Alma.

Drinking. Drinking copiously. Drinking to the point of alcohol poisoning and—for some—death.

The tragedy rocked the group. They felt heavy burdens for the teens they'd watched slip through their grasp, walking out the door to devastation and death, simply because they'd been bored on a Sunday afternoon. Because of his work with young people, LaVerne was especially affected by the tragedy. Surely there was a way to prevent such a thing from happening again.

"So he and some others got together and decided they would put out a questionnaire to find out what kids were interested in doing in the summer," says Alma. "They circulated it in schools and when they got it back the four top things were exploring river valleys, doing arts and crafts, camping, and canoeing."

The idea for a summer camp was born. The group began searching for a suitable location, and it wasn't long before the tiny hamlet of Rosebud, tucked into a cozy valley 100 kilometres northeast of Calgary—and almost completely abandoned—presented itself as the perfect answer.

Rosebud developed from unlikely beginnings. Jim Wishart, its first white settler, initially had no intention of homesteading there. He and his family were trekking through by oxcart when they stopped to camp beside Rosebud Creek. Jim emerged from his tent at sunrise, and while his wife Eliza started the fire, he gazed down the valley. What took place next must surely have seemed mystical. Thousands of brilliantly dew-dropped rosebuds blanketed the hillsides. They caught the rays of the early morning sun and glittered like jewels. The stunning sight evoked Jim's now well-documented words to Eliza:

"Here is the promised land. We go no further."

At first their only neighbour was High Eagle, a Blackfoot man who had settled his family nearby. He had been born in the midst of a raging storm. When his mother gazed up at the sky she spotted an eagle, the most sacred of all birds, floating effortlessly high above her tipi, unaffected by the weather's fury. It was a good omen, and in recognition of the blessing she named her newborn High Eagle.

High Eagle grew to be a man of peace who rose above the storm of hostilities directed towards enemy tribes, including the white man. He was a good friend and great help to the Wisharts. It was High Eagle, also known as "Wandering

Spirit of the Plains," who told them that Akokiniskway, the Blackfoot name for the valley, meant "river of many roses."

Within a decade, other homesteaders arrived, and in 1901 "Rosebud Creek" was granted a post office. Other businesses followed. When daily rail service began in 1914, business growth spiked. A general store soon joined the new hotel, a grain elevator and stockyards were added, three churches were eventually established and a hall was built. After holding classes in the hotel basement and the hall, the first school was erected in 1918.

Rosebud Creek made do with a boxcar until it received its coveted railway station in 1919, the same year Lester Cox and his wife arrived to build a barber shop and pool hall. In 1922 the word "Creek" was dropped from the post office. In the local history book, *Akokiniskway: By the River of Many Roses…*, Lester Cox recalls that the village of Rosebud was incorporated in the early 1920s, with a population of more than 200. By 1940, according to Lester, the population had reached 325. At this time a number of coal mines provided a significant boost to the economy.

Of course the residents were delighted when, just a few years earlier, the wild rose was named Alberta's official floral emblem.

Rosebud appears to have peaked in 1940. With the breakout of the Second World War, Lester and others joined the forces. Many of the wives and children who were left behind moved back home to parents and grandparents. After the war, veterans tended not to return to their old lives, instead taking advantage of the government's offer of free education and moving on. While the march of progress continued, Rosebud began to decline. In 1972 the school closed, a victim of consolidation. By 1973, only about thirty people remained. The community was fading away. That was the year, however, one person came back.

LaVerne Erickson had been a teenager in 1959 when his father, a pastor, answered a call to the Rosebud Baptist Church. Although the family only stayed two years, the charming valley left the indelible impression on them that it does on everyone who sees it. It must have felt like coming home when LaVerne realized the rolling hills and flowing river of Rosebud were the perfect setting for the summer camp he envisioned. The results of the questionnaire dovetailed with his background in art and music, and led naturally to the name of the project: Rosebud Camp of the Arts. Members of the Calgary Crescent Heights Baptist Church, the Southern Alberta Institute of Technology, and the University of Calgary came together to make the camp a reality.

"The Rosebud Mercantile was up for sale," says Alma. "They worked some things out… and acquired the use of it."

The next step was a trial camp organized for the young people of the church during Easter break in 1973. Bonita Hudson, then "just a kid in Grade Eight," will never forget it.

"Seventy-five kids between twelve and eighteen, and young adult counselors, brought out sleeping bags and three days' worth of food each, crowded into various vehicles and arrived in what we characterized as the 'ghost town' of Rosebud. [We camped] in the old general store—a rambling building, mostly empty except for a ping pong table. This area was connected to the live-in quarters, which had four bedrooms, a bathroom, a kitchen and dining area, all arranged on two levels. Other than being separated by male and female, it was wall-to-wall sleeping bags at night, with total chaos in the kitchen by day—and forget the bathroom situation. Let's say it was fortunate that there was still an outhouse in the backyard.... In the evenings we all sat on the floor in the dining area and sang campfire-type songs; in the daytimes we climbed down into Horseshoe Canyon and played a wild game of Capture the Flag. Tim Erickson [LaVerne's brother] brought a rubber raft that a few people tried to paddle down the river, and since it was spring runoff, that was chaotic. We also hiked down the railway tracks, investigated the empty houses and, when the well ran dry... we pumped water from the hand pump across the street."

By all accounts, the camp was a roaring success. With the help of a government grant, LaVerne and his supporters began planning in earnest for week-long summer camps open to young people throughout the province.

Bonita was hooked. "After that first memorable weekend," she says, "I jumped at going to camp that summer. My dad and I even went out one late May weekend to help clean up the place so it was fit for forty or so campers and counselors to stay at each week. My mom and other parents from the church youth group donated all they could of household items, such as curtains, rugs, furniture, and kitchen dishes and utensils. I don't envy the organizers sorting through all the stuff, but I'm sure it saved a pile of start-up money."

In the meantime, information was circulated through schools across the province, and Alberta Culture assisted in promoting Rosebud Camp of the Arts. Response was favourable.

"Over gravel roads from all over Alberta we travelled in small vans, parents' or counselors' vehicles," says Bonita. "The range of campers was from about age twelve to sixteen, and the counselors were about seventeen to twenty-seven years old. What a different experience! Everything was free-form. We negotiated activities from ones the counselors presented, and we were also free to suggest a few of our own."

Bonita describes the arts and crafts they did as "real": "Pottery, weaving, drawing, welding, and so on. The teachers actually were skilled in these things and I learned a lot from their experience and example. I fell in love with canoeing, but we did other things, like swim in the river, hike in the valley, and visit local landmarks, such as museums.... The prairie landscape and skyline were spectacular.... I phoned home after that first week and came back to help in the kitchen for three more weeks that summer."

Year after year the camps continued, growing ever more successful. With counselors skilled in the arts, instruction in painting, sculpture, music, and many other artforms were added. Tim Erickson, a musician as well as a natural athlete, provided a physical component to the program.

Many friendships developed and so did some romance. LaVerne met his future wife Arlene when she came to cook at the camps. His dream of Christian outreach with an emphasis on the arts was becoming reality, but Bonita is quick to point out "without his brother, wife, friends, parents, in-laws, and various relatives there wouldn't have been the moderator, experience, and the means."

Eventually Rosebud Camp of the Arts was accredited by the Alberta and Canadian Camping Associations, and the summer camps were complemented by winter weekend outings.

"Different people would rent the camp as well," recalls Alma. As word spread, groups of every kind used the facility for gatherings and retreats. Local residents began referring to it simply as "The Retreat," but although it brought new life and economy to their town, it took a long time for them to fully accept its presence in their midst.

"It's not easy for people who've been there for generations to see others come in from outside and just turn things on their heads," says Alma. "The locals didn't want camp participants to think of Rosebud as a ghost town. It's definitely not a ghost town, but it was heading that way." LaVerne and the others were aware of local sentiment and tried hard to connect with the community, even as Rosebud Camp of the Arts grew, purchasing and bringing new life to buildings that had formerly awaited demolition.

The initial dream had been realized, but the little group who started it had no idea that they had only planted a seed that was about to flower into the most magnificent rose the valley had yet seen.

The camps were so popular that some participants (and their parents) wanted more. According to Alma, several of them approached LaVerne and said, "If you ever start a school here, we'd like to come."

"So they did," she says.

The simplicity of those three little words can't possibly convey the enormity of the undertaking. Quite apart from the paperwork and other technicalities required to open a school, the venture necessitated the physical relocation to Rosebud of LaVerne and Arlene, Tim and his wife, Karla, and several others. With each empty house the new occupants moved into, a little more of the community came to life.

One of the newcomers was Alma. "We're planning to start a school. Would you be interested in coming to teach?" LaVerne asked her. They were the words Alma had wanted to hear for six years.

"I graduated in 1971 from the University of Lethbridge," she says. "I had my degree, Bachelor of Education, English major, but nobody would hire me. I was up front. I said I don't see well, and I'm classified as legally blind. And so they were very kind to me, but..." Alma was never offered a job. Her heart leapt when LaVerne demonstrated his confidence in her. "I spent about a week at Rosebud and had a look at how things were. I prayed a lot and I sensed that this was the next thing I was supposed to be doing."

Akokiniskway states that Rosebud School of the Arts "began in September 1977 with two teachers, LaVerne

Erickson, the principal, and Alma Siemens and five students. Its aim was to provide a valid alternative to the traditional public schooling with emphasis on small classes, course integration and individual challenge to expand one's horizons and moral character."

"We just called it Rosebud Centre School," says Alma. "During the first year we were not yet accredited as an official high school. Therefore the kids did correspondence courses and we were assisting. LaVerne had to wait until we were more official to design the curriculum."

Alma worked for room and board; no expenses, but no payment either. "We were a non-profit organization and that was how it started," she explains. "By then they had bought the hotel. I lived there. As well as being a teacher I was also den mom. Boys! We had only boys the first year. Four were in Grade Ten and one in Grade Twelve. That was the first semester. They all knew each other from camp. We had four more boys the second semester. The second year we started to have some girls. I moved to the upstairs area in the Rosebud Mercantile. And then I was den mom for girls."

At the end of the first year the single Grade Twelve student was honoured with a barbecue, which he attended appropriately attired in cutoffs and t-shirt.

From these humble beginnings the school grew. LaVerne's expert and imaginative guidance, combined with his emphasis on teamwork and ability to target and utilize individual talents, resulted in a well-rounded and diverse program. It ranged from an award-winning school choir, to an innovative Moral Education course, to an annual winter survival camp in the Peace country of northern Alberta.

As the fine arts high school gained momentum, the summer camps petered out. "I think the last Camp of the Arts we had was maybe one or two summers before the summer dinner theatre started," says Alma. "I guess maybe more things were happening in the city to keep the kids busy. And there wasn't as much contact with the schools anymore, because everybody was busy in Rosebud."

They certainly were: within five years, the school's population multiplied from five students to thirty and from two instructors to six—more than the former population of the entire town. People came from across North America and overseas either to attend or work at Rosebud School of the Arts.

Rosebud's 100th anniversary took place in 1983, and residents planned a huge homecoming. The School of the Arts saw the occasion as an opportunity both to strengthen ties with the community and do a little fundraising. They had no idea their plans would result in actions that virtually guaranteed Rosebud's survival and, in fact, brought it national acclaim.

Allen Desnoyers had recently joined the school staff as drama instructor, taking over from Gregg Perry, who started the program in 1981. Of the homecoming, *Akokiniskway* (which was published the same year) simply states, "The Rosebud Theatre Players presented a refreshing fif- minutes of Pre-Rosebud comedy, music and style of 16th-century Commedia del '

Fifteen minutes or not, it wa

Commedia dell'arte is a theatrical form characterized by stylized masks, comedy and improvisation, highly popular throughout Europe during the sixteenth to eighteenth centuries.

"It had stock characters," says Alma. "There was the shyster, the maiden in distress, the hero, and others. If people liked it, they threw money, and if they didn't, they threw rotten vegetables. Of course if [the actors] had creativity, they would embellish their parts and change the incidentals." Commedia dell'arte eventually evolved into other styles, such as pantomime. Characters which emerged from the commedia tradition include Punch, from Punch and Judy, and Harlequin, with his breeches and jacket of patches.

"[At the homecoming] we combined some of the madrigals and stuff we had learned from Elizabethan-type music that the students studied, and we did a little bit of stately dance," says Alma. A simple buffet dinner was also provided. Residents donated time in the kitchen, and local women were invited to sell crafts and baking.

Today, commedia dell'arte is considered a lost art, but to the good citizens of Rosebud nothing is lost. They loved the dinner theatre so much that the little troupe of players performed it again… and again… and again, throughout the summer.

"People just kept coming and sitting in our little improvised bleachers," says Alma. "It might have started out as fifteen minutes at the homecoming, but it kept getting longer and longer. It was kind of a fluid thing. People played off each other. Somebody would think of an exciting thing to say and then they'd take off in all kinds of directions. Because it was done outside, under the sky, at the end of our run in August we had to mount floodlights to shine on the stage."

Certainly no rotten vegetables sailed from the audience, and perhaps no money was thrown either, but the venture was a financial as well as a social success. "It really helped the relationship with the community," says Alma. "It definitely did that."

It was clear as well that an annual summer dinner theatre would raise much-needed funds for the school, replacing the income lost from the decline of the summer camps.

"It started as just a summer dinner theatre because it was still a high school," says Alma. But that was about to change. As the School of the Arts' summer dinner theatre became more well-known, things moved quickly. It grew from one outdoor event in the summer to three or four productions during the course of the year, and from one or two performances a week to several. Emphasis on drama at the school intensified until, in 1986, post-secondary studies in music, theatre, and Christian ministry through the creative arts were introduced. Eventually Rosebud Theatre earned professional status, and became the school's primary source of income.

In 1988 LaVerne drafted a bill which, having navigated the proper channels to the Legislature, was passed as the Rosebud School of the Arts Act, freeing the school from the auspices of Alberta Education and allowing it to create and run its own unique curriculum from Grade Seven up to a full-fledged post-secondary program.

Expansion was vital. Classrooms were needed, as well as rehearsal space, performance venues, workshops for set construction, and accommodations for students and staff. The school purchased and renovated more buildings in the formerly dying town. The hotel, once home to teacher and den mother Alma and her boys, became the school's administrative headquarters. The mercantile, once a dormitory and classrooms, became the dining room for theatregoers. The former opera house was the logical location for the theatre, but the audience had to scrunch, 150 at a time, into church pews for seating. They brought hand-held fans in summer and blankets in winter to stave off the telltale signs of the building's age. However, in 1991 the opera house was renovated, and now there is room for 220 patrons to sit in air-conditioned comfort on tiered seating with access to washrooms and a concession—a far cry from the single toilet and outhouse of the first summer camp.

Local residents couldn't help but pick up on the potential for tourism, and separate ventures emerged: Rosebud Gifts and Crafts, Rose Hip Artisan's Gift Shop, Trading Post Gallery, Rosebud Café and Folk Club, and a nine-hole golf course. The historic United Church became the Akokiniskway Art Gallery; across from the Mercantile, the Rosebud Centennial Museum now houses Little Country Blessings General Store. Rosebud Creek Recording Studio is the rehearsal hall for two community choirs as well as base for two local radio programs. Several bed and breakfast houses and other tourist accommodations are benefitting from the thousands of people who come through the community each year.

Community.

The concept was still very much on LaVerne's mind. In *Dreamers and Doers: Documentary on 100 Years of Arts and Culture in Alberta,* LaVerne states, "Our emphasis hasn't been so much on young people graduating and getting a big name in the industry. We encourage them to be entrepreneurs and to get back and work at a community level." He was gratified when local residents began enrolling in the school. There was no doubt that school and community were merging more and more.

LaVerne's message was not lost on other struggling towns. They invited him to come and speak about Rosebud's success, the marriage of art and Christianity, and the importance of building community. Such opportunities led to the 1993 development of a sister company, Chemainus Theatre, which is now the largest professional theatre on Vancouver Island.

Perhaps LaVerne had always believed that anything was possible, but his successes certainly proved it. In 1994 he realized another dream, the now-famous Canadian Badlands Passion Play, a re-enactment of the life of Christ set in a natural outdoor amphitheatre in Drumheller.

Alma recalls LaVerne's longing to stage the play in the magnificent and powerful setting—coupled with his hesitation. Here again his concern for community surfaced. "They were very careful to run it by the Jewish community,"

Alma says. "You see, in Europe, sometimes when they did Passion Plays some unholy Christians went on rampages and really made it difficult for the Jewish people. LaVerne did not want to be identified at all with that and so they made some contacts with Jewish organizations."

LaVerne cautiously termed the first performance a "pilot project," but he needn't have worried. Not only was there no backlash, but the play, which runs two weekends a year, now casts over 200 actors and utilizes approximately 1,000 volunteers from across western Canada and the northwestern United States. It spawned the development, in 1998, of yet another venture—the Canadian Badlands Performing Arts Summer School, located in Drumheller. The summer school offers a three-week accredited performing arts program for high school students who participate in the play. The Canadian Badlands Passion Play has become so celebrated that Attractions Canada recently named it Alberta's top cultural attraction, drawing tens of thousands of people to the area each year. That, along with the 50,000 who annually visit Rosebud, earned LaVerne the distinction of one of three finalists for the 2003 Ambassador Award, which recognizes individuals who make outstanding contributions to Alberta's tourism industry. In 2010 he won the award.

The Summer/Fall 2000 issue of *Futures in Focus*, a newsletter of the North Fraser Community Futures Development Corporation, states, "More than 100 people came out to hear the man that has successfully created an economic powerhouse centred around arts and culture in two communities, and has worked with dozens of others to achieve the same.... 'Communities are not built by consultants,' [LaVerne Erickson told the group], 'they are built by committed, hard-working citizens.'"

Despite being in demand far and wide, LaVerne's home and heart have remained in Rosebud. As time advanced, he and others recognized that the School of the Arts couldn't survive without the community, and the community couldn't survive without the school. The extent to which the two are inextricably bound together was dramatically demonstrated in the early 2000s when the BSE crisis (aka mad cow disease) ravaged local farming and ranching enterprises at the same time the World Trade Center attacks decimated tourism. The little community of Rosebud was crushed, for by then they relied heavily on both industries.

A press release issued by the school in 2004 announced that the school needed to raise $350,000 by the end of the year to stay afloat. It was still a non-profit charity operating almost entirely on private donations; for the first time, it now seriously sought corporate and business sponsorship. The lengthy list of current benefactors, patrons, sponsors, and donors confirms the success of the appeal.

Six years later, in 2010, construction of a new, ten-thousand-square-foot centre is underway to expand theatre facilities and provide Rosebud with a tourist information centre, thanks to the continuing support of Rosebud theatre benefactors, and federal and provincial grants dedicated to enhancing facilities and promoting and maintaining employment in rural areas. At the same time, a new fire hall is being built and the museum has undertaken renovations to meet the needs of growing numbers of tourists. In addition, the local campground has been expanded, and a fully serviced RV resort developed.

Since that horrifying day in 1973, many goals have been reached—and exceeded. Bonita Hudson is one symbol of the fruition of LaVerne's dreams. The self-described shy, dorky teenager she once was represented the youth he so desperately wanted to save from self-destruction when he started the camps; today, she represents the focus of those camps as she "learned to care for people from scary lives, with very little on the outside that made them lovable" and learned to recognize the Creator in her own creativity. Having worked summers with the Rosebud School of the Arts, this onetime "city kid" met and married a local farmer, symbolizing the linking of two distinct groups into one cohesive unit.

It is fair to say that Bonita's daughters Anna and Sarah represent the final erasure of any distinction between the Rosebud "locals" and the "outsiders." Although the two girls grew up on the farm, they worked in the tourism industry in Rosebud, at the museum, just across the street from the Mercantile where their mother vied for a spot to cram her sleeping bag with seventy-five other young people more than thirty years ago.

The final word goes to LaVerne Erickson. Or does it go to the Blackfoot, High Eagle? High Eagle too was community-minded as he welcomed and helped the outsiders who came into his land. Years later, LaVerne Erickson was the outsider, but he was equally community-minded. Just as the gently rolling coulees embrace and shelter the magnificent Rosebud Valley, LaVerne held the tiny, dying hamlet of Rosebud in his care. Like a wounded sparrow unsure of its rescuer, it bit him a few times, but ultimately recognized that he posed no threat and, indeed, only desired to help. Today the two have truly bonded, and while the population of Rosebud remains around 100, its national acclaim has assured its continued existence.

Says LaVerne, "The saga of the rejuvenation of Rosebud is still ongoing. It is one of the best-known rural communities in Canada because residents in Rosebud have grasped the significance of building community together."

Perhaps High Eagle, "Wandering Spirit of the Plains," passes by occasionally... and smiles.

Chapter 3
Big Valley

Big Valley

God and the Devil Collide

On a midwinter night in the early 1920s, the sky north of Big Valley, Alberta, glowed an ominous orange. In mere seconds the men in the community realized their greatest fear. They ran for their horses. They ran for the fire wagon. They shouted for wives to begin a coffee and sandwich brigade. Panic and adrenalin surged. The initial frenzy, however, fizzled into chaotic confusion. Where were the horses? Not a one could be found. For that matter, where were the wives? The men stood helpless as their local brothel burned to the ground.

Such a grand house, with its equally grand inhabitants. If only they could ride to the rescue of the damsels in distress. But the women of Big Valley had outwitted their men. In a furor of vigilantism, the God-fearing females had rounded up the town's horses, secured them in a hidden place, and ridden out to the sinful establishment to speed it on its way to the fires of hell. Throughout the night, scantily clad prostitutes straggled into town for refuge. Against vociferous objections, the local policeman insisted the ladies be lodged in the local hotel. In the morning they departed on the first train out. The righteous had won.

After all, Big Valley abides in God's country. The story goes that God raced to finish creating the ranges east of Highway 56 before Sunday, His day of rest. But He fell short of the goal. While He rested on the Sabbath, His ever-scheming nemesis took matters into his own hands. When God returned to his handiwork Monday morning, He was shocked to find a gleeful Beelzebub snickering over a deliberately botched job. Ever afterward it was said that Alberta's Highway 56 divides God's country from the devil's.

Being on God's side of the line has been a blessing for the village of Big Valley, located in the centre of the province. Since the community's inception in 1907, it has lived through two booms and two busts, and still it carries on. Today, with a population of 340—a quarter its former numbers—the village continues to thrive. God giveth and God taketh away, but God also hath a sense of humour, which He amply imparted to the people of this dynamic little town, who live by the motto that God helps those who help themselves.

The riches of the earth surrounding Big Valley were generous, first to the ranchers, who began arriving around 1900, attracted by waist-high grass perfect for grazing.

Among them was Pat Burns, founder of the largest meatpacking company in western Canada.

In 1905 the railroad arrived in Stettler, thirty kilometres to the north, and the Big Valley area was opened to settlers. The era of free land was in full swing. For a ten-dollar patent fee, any man could claim title over his own quarter section. People of every race, religion, and colour came through the Stettler Dominion Land Office. Magistrate Billy Grey reached into his own pockets to ensure that even the destitute got their share. A spirit of friendly cooperation prevailed, due in large part to the ranchers, who were by now accustomed to helping their neighbours in every situation.

Some of the settlers saw an opportunity to secure their livelihoods by giving back. Homesteaders travelling to Stettler for supplies, and ranchers trailing herds to the railroad, faced a tiresome round trip of at least three days. To provide respite and basic goods, entrepreneurs set up stopping places and stores along the way.

The land yielded more of its treasures with soft coal, perfect for heating homes. To begin with, ranchers, farmers, and business owners simply helped themselves, digging and hauling coal from the banks of the Red Deer River. Neighbours assisted one another, as it took two teams of horses to negotiate the steep banks. The first coalmine opened in 1908. In time, Big Valley was skirted by up to a dozen mines. The black resource was so plentiful that the mere act of digging a posthole could reveal a seam, which is exactly how the valley's largest mine, Big Valley Collieries, made its beginnings.

In 1910 and 1911, the Canadian Northern Railway laid track south from Stettler, bringing the first freight train to Big Valley in 1911. Business was brisk. Town lots sold and homesteads were snapped up. At least one of the merchants along the trail moved his business into the community. Two general stores were established, along with two implement dealers and an agency for McLaughlin cars. Two restaurants, a post office, a telephone operator, a livery barn, and a meat market were in business. A blacksmith's shop, a hardware store, a lumberyard, and a grain elevator soon followed.

A mile and a half north of the community, Big Valley Collieries spread like wildfire, expanding from eleven employees to forty-five in little more than a year. In time the company built a three-storey hotel accommodating one hundred employees next to the mine, and a school for the children of miners with families.

A railway station was constructed in the town in 1912, and passenger service commenced six days a week. Canadian Northern Railway's decision to base their terminal in Big Valley sealed the community's good fortune. Construction crews flooded in to raise a roundhouse, railyards, a water tower, a pumphouse, a coal dock, maintenance shops, and stockyards. When they left they were replaced by railmen. Roundhouse crews, bridge and building crews, engine crews, station employees, track repair gangs, and other railroaders set up residence. With the dramatic increase in population, more businesses opened, including one of central Alberta's finest hotels. By 1914, there were fifteen trains running out of the community and, with the election of councillors,

Big Valley was officially named a village. By the time it graduated to town status in 1920 it had all the amenities of a big city, and its population had surged to 1,025. There was no looking back—or so the residents thought.

A significant percentage of the influx consisted of young, single men working the railroads and the mines. The community met their *needs* admirably with a tennis court, baseball diamonds, golf course, curling rink, and skating rink. The men's *desires*, however, were another matter. When an enterprising madam came through town and spotted the plenitude of virile young men, ripe for the picking, she recognized an opportunity for a roaring trade. She built a house north of the community and moved in her ladies of the night.

The residents of Big Valley were a lively bunch who made it their business to have fun—good, clean, or otherwise. The newly formed Athletic Association made a perfect cover for games of chance. The only equipment needed was a deck of cards and a pocketful of cash. Several other gambling joints flourished as well. Moonshining enjoyed a profitable trade. Incredibly, enforcement of the law fell on the shoulders of only one man. Policeman Della Torre's judiciously blind eye miraculously saw the light only if harm to life and limb was ﹍inent.

It was high times in the big valley, but as history (and the Good Book) repeatedly warns us, good times often portend a fall. In 1919, the Canadian Northern Railway and several other railway companies amalgamated to form the Canadian National Railway. In 1924, to better accommodate its expanding web of track, the new CNR announced that Mirror, Alberta would make a more suitable divisional point than Big Valley. The so-called "Battle of Big Valley" resulted in the relocation of the roundhouse and associated facilities, the transfer of railmen to other points, and Big Valley fighting a bitter, losing war to maintain its status and its population as a railway town. The rail line that once brought prosperity to Big Valley now drew it away. Rural people rode newly laid steel to different market towns. This loss of commerce, as well as the loss of railmen and their families, spelled death for several Big Valley businesses.

To compound the problem, the following year Big Valley Collieries drastically decreased its coal output. Production continued to decline until the collieries closed in 1927. Though it had yet to cast its pall over the prairies, the Great Depression of the 1930s visited Big Valley early. By 1929, the beleaguered town owed $7,000 on its school, teachers were resigning and more businesses were leaving, taking population and tax dollars with them. When the dry years of the Depression did hit, they hit hard. More railmen were laid off and more businesses closed. By 1932, as many as 100 houses had been moved out of Big Valley and the population had shrunk to 447, less than half that of its glory years. Farmers and ranchers who had purch land during the good times discovered they owed more than their land was worth. Foreclosures abounded. Many of the afflicted loaded their scant belongings onto wagons, trucks, or Bennett buggies and headed for the new "promised land" in northern Alberta's Peace River country. Between 1930 and 1939, ten Big Valley businesses were lost to fire. One can only speculate as to why.

After the depression Big Valley continued to experience hard times. Increased automation and paved highways took people to Stettler and other larger centres to shop. If water seepage, poor structure, and inferior product quality didn't close the mines, a diminishing need for coal did. A few new mines opened, but they didn't last long. When in 1956, after 30 years of operation, Big Valley's longest-running mine was declared abandoned, citizens finally conceded the end of the coal mining era.

The boom was officially bust. Now a shadow of its former self, Big Valley simply rested, like many other small communities on the prairies. The elevators, post office, and school quietly served the people of the area, but there was no new growth. By 1974, only a skeleton railway crew remained, the population had further dwindled to 300 and the town was once again a village.

Contrary to appearances, however, it was not dying. Like a moth in a cocoon, it was silently transforming into a butterfly. From 1950 onward, the area had been the site of oil and gas exploration. Within three decades, Big Valley was booming again.

Ironically, the discovery of fossil fuels took place due to an act of God. In the late 1940s a blizzard forced seismic operations in the foothills to move east. Work resumed near Stettler and oil was discovered in the Big Valley area. The hunt for more oil was on and the finds were fabulous. The "Big Valley No. 7" discovery well opened in 1950. Further development resulted in the now-famous Fenn-Big Valley Field, which ultimately produced more than 321 million barrels of oil and 85 billion cubic feet of gas. By the time the swell peaked in the mid-1980s, up to nineteen rigs were in full swing, and the town was thriving again. Big Valley sorely missed the 100 dwellings it had seen leave town in the first bust. Housing was so scarce that oil and gas workers and their families lived in granaries dragged into town from surrounding farms. But spirits were high as long as oil and money flowed. At the height of the boom, well sites around Big Valley produced 26 per cent of Gulf Canada's light oil, and similar amounts for Shell and Esso.

History, however, was about to repeat itself. Inevitably, oil and gas reserves depleted. The gush became a stream, the stream became a trickle, and most of the wells tapped out. Though some exploration continues, oil companies moved crews and equipment away, leaving Big Valley bereft once more.

Today a fraction of the fuel deposits remain, as does a fraction of the population. The final blows occurred when the railway stopped service altogether and the elevator closed. Area farmers had to haul their grain elsewhere, so of course they shopped elsewhere, taking further business, population, and tax dollars away from the town. Even stable, long-term strongholds like the Royal Bank, which had been in town since 1913, finally pulled up stakes.

Big Valley was in big trouble. What did they have left? The coal was gone, the oil was gone, the gas was gone, train and elevator service were gone, and most of the people were gone. It seemed all that was left were memories of the glory days. Memories.

What happened next separates towns that survive from those which die. The people of Big Valley had a eureka moment. Why not capitalize on their past to secure their future? Yes, the elevator was closed, but it was still there. So were the railyards and the roundhouse, albeit in ruins. The Canadian National Railway had sold most of their abandoned track for salvage, but the section running from Big Valley to Stettler remained. The East Central Alberta Heritage Society had purchased and rented it to the Stettler-based Alberta Prairie Steam Tours. Their unique railway excursion packages, offering junkets in old-fashioned coaches pulled by restored steam- or diesel-powered locomotives, were gaining rapid popularity. Passengers who thought they were purchasing a ticket for a tranquil, scenic train ride from Stettler to Big Valley and back were treated to a few surprises along the way, including a shoot-'em-up train robbery by a gang of pistol-toting, horsebacked hooligans; a near-hijacking of someone's husband by a gunslinging, man-seeking Wild West "Calamity Jane," and a heroic rescue by the historic "Gabriel Dumont."

The fact that Big Valley's historic 1912 railway station was the destination point for the excursions fired the citizens' imaginations. Big Valley had a colourful history too. No one was too proud to use it to create a tourist attraction of their own. Almost all of the approximately 300 remaining residents got involved as they picked up the theme of the excursions and ran with it.

Today when a train rolls into town, it is greeted by a platform full of smiling townspeople dressed in period costume, waving a welcome to the arriving passengers. Then they bustle off to their various businesses and station themselves for the onslaught of tourist dollars coming through their doors.

At the site of one of Big Valley's early Chinese restaurants is the Jimmy Jock Boardwalk, named after the restaurateur himself. The horseshoe-shaped walk is designed to look like the main street of a frontier town. Early Big Valley establishments have been resurrected there, including the infamous House of Ill Repute. Behind their false fronts are legitimate businesses: a tea room, a fudge factory, a saloon, a barber shop, an antiques and collectibles shop, and art galleries. Even the crude, tiny jailhouse, built in 1914, is back in action for the tourists' amusement. Passengers from the train enjoy a self-guided walking tour which takes them through the roundhouse ruins, the railyards, and other carefully maintained historic sites.

God and the devil are at it again. The Big Valley Creation Science Museum, the first of its kind in Canada, unflinchingly claims that evolution is a lie and sets out to prove it. Despite (or perhaps because of) the controversial nature of the museum's mission, people travel from thousands of kilometres away just to see it.

In its quest to offer visitors as many attractions as possible, Big Valley acquired the physical component of the Canadian Railway Hall of Fame (a virtual, web-based entity). Visitors can roam through the outdoor Hall of

Fame pavilion, learning about the historic and ongoing importance of the railway industry in Canada, and those who played key roles in its influence upon the nation.

Big Valley succeeded in saving its elevator from demolition by having it designated a historic resource. It stands near the train station, which functions again, not just for excursion passengers, but as a museum showcasing the town's history and the area's railway heritage.

The residents of Big Valley pulled as much of their history out of the past as they could, presenting it to the world warts and all. They even took advantage of the blooper of 1974, when a desperate homecoming committee, eager to spruce up the town but short on funds, didn't think twice about snatching up a volume of unclaimed paint from the local lumber yard to freshen up St. Edmund's Anglican Church. (Can you hear the devil snickering?) The beautiful church, which sits prominently on the hill overlooking the town, was built in 1916, thanks to a generous endowment from a British woman who had never been to Canada. But it was faded and weather-beaten and showing its age. By the time parishioners caught wind of the painting plot, it was too late: the church, formerly white, was now a dazzling robin's-egg blue. At first the Anglicans were upset, but it soon became clear that the hilltop building, unused since the 1960s, was now so outstanding that the sight of it drew people in off the highway. Requests to use the church for weddings and other occasions began coming in. Today Big Valley's affectionately christened "Blue Church" is owned by the historical society and is a favourite tourist attraction. To add to its appeal, a resident donated a bell-ringing device for the steeple which automatically tolls out every hour, lending additional quaint charm to the community.

At a designated hour, passengers from the excursion train meet in the Big Valley community hall, where they're served a home-cooked meal along with a helping of local theatre entertainment. The actors keep things lively by drawing unsuspecting tourists into their shenanigans.

Eventually the "all aboard" call sounds from the station and the passengers embark to return to Stettler. They take back what they leave behind: smiling faces, a strong sense of history, and feelings of goodwill and well-being.

Each year, twenty-five to thirty thousand people come through Big Valley in this manner, eager to spend their tourist dollars. These passengers are not the bedraggled, burned-out painted ladies, so revered by the coalminers and railroaders and so reviled by the righteous women of the town. Their departure from the same station ninety years ago was a forlorn one. How could they have known that almost a century later they would be instrumental in reviving a failing town? The righteous women would be outraged. Ironically, so would the devil!

Chapter 4
Neubergthal

Neubergthal

One Street Town

It's tempting to draw parallels between the Biblical Moses and Johann Klippenstein. Both men set out at an advanced age on long, grueling journeys to lead their people from oppression to a promised land. Both succeeded, but neither set foot on the destination. Moses' story hardly needs retelling; Klippenstein's may be less familiar.

In 1875, sixty-five-year-old Johann Klippenstein knew he'd reached his sunset years in Bergthal Colony, South Russia, yet still he dreamed of establishing a village in a land where, finally, his people would be allowed the right not to kill another human being. As a Mennonite, pacifism, the separation of church and state, Christianity with an emphasis on adult baptism, and communal living were cornerstones of his faith. Since the establishment of the Mennonite community during the sixteenth century, the group had suffered mass migrations, trailing from the Netherlands to West Prussia (Poland) and finally to South Russia (Ukraine), enduring broken promises and persecution in an elusive search for freedom of religion and education.

They'd been in Russia only a century when the government decided to press Mennonite males into military service and enforce the Russian language in Mennonite schools. The weary signs of oppression weighed down upon them once more, and the Mennonites looked for yet another land to call home.

In the meantime, Canada's own survival was threatened. In 1875, large portions of its vast landscape remained unsettled, making it vulnerable to American annexation. In response, Canadian officials rushed to establish settlers on Canadian soil. They were more than happy to welcome the Mennonites, a people whose work ethic and farming expertise were well known, and who would break, tame, and help populate the land.

Canada's offer to the Mennonites was attractive. Under the Homestead Act, in exchange for residing on and working the land for three years, all males over 21 would receive 160 free acres and be assured of the right to worship freely, operate their own schools, and refrain from military service. In an unprecedented gesture, the Canadian government also agreed to set aside large blocks of land (reserves) specifically for Mennonite settlement, so members could live and farm near one another, as was their custom. Such a gesture had never before been offered a group of immigrants, though it would later be repeated for Icelandic settlers, and many Mennonites found new hope in the prospect of the Canadian prairies.

Johann Klippenstein was one of them, and he made plans to move his entire family from Russia to southern Manitoba. The trip was onerous. Over two slow months they travelled, first by ship, then by train, and finally horse and wagon, to join fellow Mennonites in the first block settlement, east of the Red River. By this time early Mennonite immigrants had identified a problem: the large reserves of land they had negotiated in order to preserve their sense of community actually wound up eroding it. The standard 160-acre plots (quarter sections) surveyed for settlement throughout the prairies were square. The parcels were indeed side-by-side, allowing Mennonites to live and farm next to one another, but they couldn't easily help or visit each other, or even see the homesteads of their brethren. Churches and schools were not easily accessible.

Throughout their history Mennonites had lived and worked communally, in street villages: narrow, elongated farms placed side-by-side along a single street. Their orchards, pastures, and crops stretched out in long ribbons behind their yards, often fringeing the banks of a common river. Although each family was economically independent, they all worked the land, butchered and baked together. Churches and schools were built opposite one another in the centre of the village. Help and human contact were only steps away.

The Canadian quarter section system was a setback.

Before long, Mennonites began pooling land allotments and setting up street villages. The Canadian government, anxious to accommodate the new settlers, amended the Homestead Act to allow Mennonites their unique pattern of settlement.

Johann Klippenstein brought his family and his dreams as far as the street village of Rosenthal in the East Reserve. He died there in 1877, but by then his children had taken up the torch. Two sons and two daughters, along with their families and others, were hard at work establishing a street village across the Red River on the West Reserve. They named it Neubergthal, in memory of their Russian birthplace.

The West Reserve consisted of treeless grassland that the surveyors had considered uninhabitable. But they hadn't counted on the agrarian skills of the Mennonites, who immediately planted rows of trees on either side of what is now Highway 421. "The Russian cottonwood was brought over in seed form from Russia," says Margruite Krahn, an artist living in Neubergthal today. "At times the seeds from both the cottonwoods and flower and vegetable gardens were sewn into the hems of clothing, as they were not allowed into the country."

Many of these trees remain today, tall and mighty. Along with Manitoba maples, willows, and evergreens, they are a stunning, startling reminder that with hard work and caring hands, civilization can be wrought on a vast, empty plain. Less than a kilometre was required to lay out more than thirty neat, orderly farms, roughly ten acres each, with dwellings an even twenty-four metres from the road. In the space between the houses and the tree-lined street, masses of flowers were planted in large gardens. Extending behind the houses were pastures and cropland. Not only did this uniquely uniform pattern bring order and beauty to the untamed prairie, but it also reinforced Mennonite principles of community and equality. The remaining pooled quarter sections were parceled out in such a way that the best and worst farmland was divided equally, and each farmer had roughly the same distance to travel to reach his fields. There were no fences. Individual properties and fields were delineated only by narrow strips of grass.

The theme of community harmony and equality was further reflected in the local architecture. After making do with sod shacks for a couple of years while they established their footing on the land, Mennonites turned to building traditional "housebarns," in which house and barn were joined, flowing together under one long roofline. Housebarns extended perpendicularly from the street, so that front doors didn't face the road; they faced the neighbour. Back and front doors were placed roughly parallel. "They created very strong connections through features like this," relates Dr. Mary Anne Beecher, of the University of Manitoba. "If every house in the village opened its doors at the same time, you could look through all of them from one end of the village to the other."

Housebarns were practical and efficient on many levels. To milk cows or tend horses, one simply opened a door and stepped into the barn, like slipping into another room. It's staggering to consider the number of accidents that might have been mitigated, or lives saved, had housebarns been a standard feature of all prairie settlement. Deadly incidents in which people got lost between buildings during a blizzard or met with a barn accident too far from the house for their cries for help to be heard would have been virtually unknown.

Housebarns provided other practical conveniences as well, such as economical heat exchange between the two areas. The need for long, uncomfortable treks to the outhouse was eliminated by the installation of seats in the barn above gutters down which animal waste was routinely cleansed. The first indoor bathroom did not appear in Neubergthal until the 1960s.

One might think of this way of living as unsanitary. In fact, the opposite is true. Mennonite immigrants were fastidiously clean. Housebarns were built on raised mounds to protect them from flooding and kept in pristine condition. Barn walls were regularly whitewashed. The barn was such an integral part of the house that most family members and visitors came and went through the barn door instead of the house door. As farmers became more prosperous, dwellings were built with a passageway linking the house and barn. This area was often used as a summer kitchen during warm months and could also be used for sleeping.

The layout of the houses reflected the communal tone of the village. A typical two-room house would be dominated by a huge central oven extending into each room. More rooms were then added according to need and wealth, in a more or less circular arrangement around the locus of the oven. Up to six rooms were connected by doorways, not hallways, allowing for a smooth, continuous flow of movement throughout the house. Each room served several purposes. Bedrooms were almost nonexistent, as any space could be used for sleeping. Because of this, Mennonite furniture was often multi-functional, collapsible and portable. Parents slept in the formal parlour, which was also used to entertain guests. Their bed doubled as storage space on which good linens were piled during the day. The kitchen was the busiest room in the house. Much more than a place to prepare and eat food, it served as a workshop, as well as an area for informal visiting. During the day, the warm cubby atop the oven served as a bed for infants or sick children. At night the kitchen doubled as sleeping quarters for children or hired help. It wasn't uncommon to sleep four or five to a room, except in the case of newlyweds, who were given their own. Sleeping benches were used as regular benches during the day. Some were chests with hinged lids. Older girls and young children slept towards the centre of the house near the oven while older boys slept on the perimeter, a reflection of the way Mennonites viewed the woman's role as being in the home while men dealt with the outside world. Similarly, most houses had a floor-to-ceiling cabinet with glass doors above and drawers below built right into an interior wall, which women used to display family treasures and store fine linens. Opposite it, mounted on an outside wall, was the men's cupboard, with a solid door behind which "worldly" items like accounts, passports, money, tobacco, and alcohol were hidden from view. These items, accessible only to the head male, symbolized his power and independence in the household. Beneath this cupboard a table displayed the family Bible, a reminder of God's supreme authority.

Due to a dearth of wood on the West Reserve, homes were heated with slabs of cow manure mixed with straw and dried in storage. They provided a slow, odourless heat which circulated throughout the house over walls that didn't quite reach the ceiling. An additional source of heat came from the barn, which not only protected one end of the house from the elements, but emitted heat from the animals as well.

Horse manure, mixed with mud and chaff, made durable, insulating plaster for walls. Once applied, it was whitewashed with lime. The fire-resistant plaster was extremely strong—to the point where restorers a century later needed an electric chipper to chisel through what they compared to "soft concrete."

Houses were generally white; barns were red. Interior colours were many and varied. Pastel greens, blues, pinks and lavender were set off with bright matching trim. A popular base colour for floors was ochre. Since houses were the women's domain they did all the painting. In a communal environment it was one of the few areas in which individual creativity shone. In almost every house wooden floors—especially in the kitchen—were painted with beautifully designed "carpets," intricately patterned and meticulously applied. Each was unique. Using a board as a straight edge, stencils, brushes, and sponges cut with designs and a minimum of three colours, women gave their artistry free rein, producing stunning recreations of Persian-style rugs. Over the years, floral designs evolved into patterns of interweaving lines and geometric shapes articulated with great precision. It's almost unfortunate that linoleum appeared by the early 1930s, gradually covering these works of art. A major endeavour of restorers and archivists today is recovering and preserving the Mennonite "rugs."

Mennonite families were large and houses were often crowded. It wasn't unusual for up to a dozen people, ranging from infants to grandparents to hired hands, to live in one house. Unless there were newlyweds temporarily living with parents, only the elderly were given their own room, a symbol of the degree of respect they commanded within the household. Babies slept with parents; older girls slept with younger children; older boys slept on the periphery of the house—in the passageway to the barn or perhaps in the barn lean-to or loft. When children married, they often moved in with one set of parents while saving money to buy their own land and build their own housebarn. Even after marrying, the youngest child typically stayed in the birth home to look after aging parents and eventually take over the farm. An explosion of weddings took place in Neubergthal between 1910 and 1920, and overcrowding became critical. Families began converting second stories into bedrooms. This space had previously been used for storage, especially of grain, which provided the house with an extra layer of insulation. The space was unheated, extremely cold in winter and hot in summer, but there was little choice but to utilize it.

Despite the overcrowded conditions, family bonds flourished and, perhaps because roles were so well-defined, conflict was rare. A fundamental principle of the community and their faith was looking out for one another. The entire community hayed, threshed, butchered, baked, worshipped, played, celebrated, and grieved together. Paths and trails threading between houses sewed them together like a patchwork quilt. Poorer families who didn't farm (such as the village herdsman, who oversaw a communal pasture consisting of 20 per cent of village land; teachers; tradesmen; widows, and the unmarried elderly) were reasonably looked after by the wealthier members of the community. In the early 1900s, a store opened in Neubergthal in a portion of a barn. It soon expanded to its own location to carry groceries and general merchandise.

It was common for families to hire help for the house and farm. These were often people from poorer households who moved into their employers' homes. They stayed at least until the youngest children turned six, old enough to begin doing chores and start school.

Village life revolved around religious worship and education. Over time there have been three schools in the centre of the village. Until compulsory attendance was legislated, Mennonite children went to school only until age twelve. Reading, writing, and arithmetic were important, but only insofar as they provided the necessary skills to read religious texts and properly run a farm. Teachers were generally not professionally trained, and often farmed part-time. They were given living quarters on school property, along with pasture for livestock.

The cemetery was next to the school. There was no church in Neubergthal for many years. This wasn't much of a problem, though, as almost all residents travelled to nearby Sommerfeld to worship, and funerals and weddings traditionally took place in homes. It wasn't until 1937 that members began worshipping locally. They first met in the home and barn of a resident. Then, in 1944, they built a church. The building looked much like a regular house on the outside, a throwback to days in Russia, where Mennonites had been forbidden to publicize their religion by worshipping in buildings that looked like churches. They differentiated churches from houses by building them parallel to the street, rather than perpendicular to it.

The Neubergthal church was torn down in 1969 as members joined other Mennonite churches in the area. Two years earlier, the school had suffered the same fate. In 1973, the store closed. But in fact, Neubergthal had begun to fade long before that. In 1880, there had been approximately 95 street villages in southern Manitoba. That number increased to more than 120 by 1900, but within twenty-five years of their inception, street villages began to die. The reasons were varied and cumulative. Street villages had never been recognized as a conventional settlement pattern in Canada, so their existence was tenuous to begin with. Also, even though the Mennonites as a society held themselves apart from the outside world, they still needed to trade and do commerce with it. Canada was a new country, only ten years old, when the Mennonites arrived. In previous migrations they'd had to pit their culture against an already existing one, but in Canada they were on the cusp of a developing new culture. The persecution they'd suffered for hundreds of years was no longer an issue, and the need to band together to defend themselves against it evaporated. A glitch occurred in 1918 when the Manitoba government forced Mennonite schools to conform to the public school curriculum, which mandated instruction in English and didn't include religion. Some Mennonite families emigrated to Paraguay and Mexico in protest, but those who stayed circumvented the School Act by offering German and religion classes half an hour before and after the prescribed school day. Like many other homesteaders of every background and ethnicity, they pulled older boys from school each fall and spring for a few weeks to help with harvest and seeding.

Aside from a few temporary tensions experienced by a number of ethnic groups during the First World War, there were no other strictures on the Mennonites. They could live where they wanted, purchase as much land as they liked, engage in commerce with anyone they chose, join professional guilds, and practice their religious beliefs without fear. Within a generation, Mennonite males were opting to move out of street villages and buy and farm land on their own. Some had no choice, as available land surrounding the village became scarce.

As the street village farmers quickly became prosperous, more horses and equipment crowded their farms. Then, as automation introduced mechanized implements too large and unwieldy for narrow strips of farmland, Mennonite farmers inevitably grew out of their street villages. As the physical structure of the villages dissolved, so, gradually, did communal living. Cultural symbols, such as style of clothing, house orientation, and gender-assigned roles fell by the wayside. It became acceptable to hang family photographs and scripture verses on walls that were formerly devoid of anything but a calendar; weddings took place in churches, with the bride in white instead of black. As residents died or left, housebarns were torn down, moved, used for storage, or abandoned. Conventional, modern housing took their place. In short, while they retained their religious beliefs, Mennonites became absorbed into mainstream society. It is significant that, for once, the choice was theirs, rather than something that was imposed upon them by a ruling authority.

Some street villages expanded into conventional prairie towns, while others dwindled into nothing but a stretch of trees along a lonely road. Today, only eighteen street villages remain, and of those, only Neubergthal strives to preserve its cultural heritage.

Ironically, the village wasn't seeking recognition or revitalization when Parks Canada took an interest in 1989. "The Historic Sites and Monuments Board was looking to preserve agricultural settlements of the prairies," says Krahn. "They shortlisted a couple of Mennonite street villages in the area, and Neubergthal won the designation."

The approximately 100 people who lived there felt dubious. They were quite happy with their laid-back, peaceful existence and weren't sure they wanted it disrupted.

They did, however, recognize that they'd inherited a valued, dying culture, and that Parks Canada was giving them the chance to reclaim it and show it to the world. Therein lay the conundrum. Traditional Mennonites shied away from worldly matters and attention of any kind. They were quiet, orderly people who valued privacy and conservatism. The idea of their village becoming a National Historic Site and having tourists descend upon it was unsettling. But it was also gratifying to know that their culture was respected to the point where Canada wanted to honour and preserve it. The villagers in Neubergthal knew they represented something special and needed to decide if they would share it with the world. "It was with mixed feelings that the community agreed," states Krahn.

The designation marked a halt to Neubergthal's slow descent into oblivion and the beginnings of a gradual ascent back to awareness. Serious research into the history and lifestyle of their immigrant ancestors commenced. Further alteration or destruction of original buildings and traditional landscapes ceased, and planning for active preservation began. Frieda Esau Klippenstein, a Parks Canada historian with ties to Neubergthal, solidified the research in *A Cultural Landscape History: Neubergthal National Historic Site: A Mennonite Street Village on the Canadian Prairie*, published in 1997. As the liaison between Parks Canada and Neubergthal, Klippenstein also worked on cost-sharing strategies for future site projects. A Neubergthal Heritage Foundation board was established and the first major restoration began: a 1901 housebarn complete with original clay brick oven. It now functions as an interpretive centre and working model of a historic Mennonite home, in which visitors are served traditional homemade bread, jam, and pickles.

Canada Day 2000 was an appropriate date for the descendents of the area's original settlers to flock back for a huge homecoming. The village swelled to three times its size for the occasion. In the midst of skits, dancing, music, stories, and general revelry, attendees gathered in the old schoolyard to witness the unveiling of a permanent plaque officially declaring Neubergthal a National Historic Site. There was no turning back.

But residents needn't have worried that their peaceful lives would be disrupted by the change. If anything, the opposite turned out to be true.

"The designation has moved some of us to a more traditional way of life," says Krahn. "We bake in the Russian bake oven, are mindful of planting trees and gardens in a more traditional manner, and are interested in preservation of not only buildings but stories."

The village remains charming and serene, with its many trees, orchards, and flower and vegetable gardens planted in predictable, orderly sequence. Properties are neatly kept, and speak of industriousness and a self-sustaining lifestyle.

While through its pysical environment the village strives to replicate what life was like between 1870 and 1940, Krahn points out that villagers have not reverted to the religious conservatism or communal lifestyle of original Neubergthal settlers. The population is eclectic, only eight housebarns remain standing, and the land formerly worked by nearly 40 farmers is now managed by a scant few. "But the feel and look is there," says Krahn. "And there is a sense of calm and order."

If Neubergthal had not drawn national attention, it almost certainly would have died. Twenty years ago, most of the residents still held kinship ties to the original settlers and to each other. Today fewer than half can make that claim. With elderly descendents passing on and others moving to centres with more services, the population should have dropped dramatically. Yet it has remained stable. A fascinating variety of people are attracted to Neubergthal. They include historians, architecture buffs, people seeking a more self-sustaining, environmentally friendly lifestyle, and others who simply want a peaceful rural existence.

"My neighbour across the road, originally from Waterloo, Ontario, bought the house portion of an 1880s housebarn because of the history and architecture," says Krahn. "[Alternatively,] some of the more conservative Mennonite sects are drawn to the village because they sense the Mennonite culture through the physical landscape. A Huldeman school and church started in the last 10 years and is beginning to draw people to the village."

Krahn herself came from Winnipeg with her husband Paul and two daughters in 1998. "We were involved in a book study group, reading a book by Wendell Berry called *What Are People For?* The book had a strong emphasis on the importance of preserving one's culture, an agrarian lifestyle and a less destructive way of living on the land. One of the women in the group grew up in Neubergthal and suggested we take a trip to a place very much like what Berry was writing about. We fell in love with the place."

Today Krahn is the chair of the Neubergthal Heritage Foundation. She and Paul, an English teacher, renovated a barn into living quarters and her art studio. The former herdsman's house also sits on their property. The only herdsman's house left standing in Canada, it retains its original beamed ceiling and painted floor. In 2002, it was designated a Manitoba Municipal Heritage Site. "My husband and I are restoring it, thanks to grants from Culture, Heritage and Tourism." Once restored, it will be available as a guest house for tourists. Other restorations in the works are a stackwall house and an 1876 housebarn, which will ultimately be an education and resource centre.

But progress is slow and funding is an ongoing issue. "We do not take out loans," says Krahn. "We depend solely on grants and donations. I find this daunting at times."

Manitoba Culture, Heritage and Tourism is assisting with the stackwall house, but according to Krahn, the housebarn will be a $600,000 project. "I'm optimistic we'll get the funds," she says, "but it takes time."

Time might be a blessing in disguise, as longtime residents adjust to the newfound limelight and tourists traipsing through their backyards—metaphorically if not literally. "There are some residents who feel there is a lot more traffic in the village and that vehicles get in the way of the farm implements," says Krahn. She points out, however, that there is as much traffic from the new Huldeman church and school as there is tourist traffic. "Having said all this," she adds, "the Neubergthal Heritage Foundation almost always works to keep the people of the village in mind."

The future of Neubergthal looks bright. Acquisition of more buildings with a view to further restoration is planned, and a website was recently launched.

Neubergthal's past has provided a launching point into its future. The community's continuing survival depends upon its preservation of traditional architecture and lifestyles. The fact that residents are seeking simpler, more self-sustaining lifestyles, according to Mennonite precepts, is attracting like-minded people to the village. The evolving population may not all be Mennonite, but they all acknowledge and respect Mennonite culture, and seek to emulate many of the Mennonite ways.

Since they became a distinct society 500 years ago, the Mennonites have been consistently rejected by every country they've wanted to call home. In Canada, they finally found a land that not only accepted them, but honoured them. Neubergthal is the living proof.

Chapter 5
Craik

Craik

The Power Of Straw

If towns were compared to comic book characters, Craik, in south-central Saskatchewan, would be Superman. Just as Clark Kent's unassuming appearance disguises the muscular crimefighter underneath, Craik's humble façade of aging buildings and unpaved streets belie a powerful, life-changing force that resonates throughout the world. This tiny town of fewer than 500 people is not only saving itself, it's helping save the planet.

"The whole thing started as a way to get two more families to move to Craik," says resident Aaron Obrigewitsch, "and it just kind of mushroomed from there."

The town has always been small. Though it was incorporated more than a century ago, in 1907, its population has never surpassed 800. By 2001, fewer than that resided in the municipality and town combined. When only 418 remained in the village, Craik's slow decline had reached a crisis point.

"We still had a doctor, a pharmacy, and a school," says Aaron. "But if we lost five people we could lose all that. If we lost the doctor, we'd lose the pharmacist. If we lost some kids, we'd probably lose a teacher. We were at a precipice."

"We lost a grocery store," remarks retired town administrator Shirley Eade. "We lost a hardware store. We opened a new hospital and the very next year it was demoted to a health centre. We needed something to keep our community alive. We needed a future.

"We'd been working with the Midlakes Community Coalition, which is a group of people along Highway 11 who got together in the early 1980s as a think tank to decide how we can sustain ourselves out here," says Shirley. The Coalition opted, with some success, to promote regional tourism. They had the highway renamed Louis Riel Trail, and communities from Hanley to Lumsden got busy developing tourist attractions based on history and recreation. But by 2001, for Craik and the surrounding district, it wasn't enough.

Enter Lynn Oliphant, University of Saskatchewan professor emeritus and dedicated environmentalist. After many years of working to reverse the effects of environmental abuse, Lynn realized that the only way to bring about change was to target the source of the problem: human beings. He'd already made great strides in reducing his own ecological footprint. Now he set about educating and encouraging others to do the same. As the world prepared to enter the new millennium, he and some colleagues founded the Prairie Institute for Human Ecology to research and teach sustainable living practices. Lynn saw huge potential for establishing self-sustaining eco-villages on the prairies where space is vast and resources plentiful. He approached town after town with his crusading vision. Many expressed support for the concept, but none were prepared to impose such a drastic paradigm shift upon their own community.

Then he attended a Midlakes Community Coalition meeting. "They said he should talk to the town," says Aaron. "So he came to our next joint Town-RM meeting and his timing was pretty good, because we had just been talking about what we were going to do."

The councils of the two governing bodies were receptive—so much so that the RM offered 127 acres of land just east of the community for development of the project.

"We formed a committee, put our heads together, and talked about the eco-village," says Shirley. It seems incredible that an area with such a small population would even consider a grand scale project like this. But Craik had achieved the seemingly insurmountable before.

"Craik was one of the first two municipalities in the province to have medicare," she says, "back in the twenties when the province hadn't thought about it. It hired its own doctor and looked after its own people." Indeed, to this day, Craik hires and takes responsibility for all the needs of its doctor, just to ensure it continues to have one. That the indomitable blood of its pioneers has coursed down through the generations is evidenced by Shirley's quick reaction to the subject of current trends towards school closures and consolidations. "We absolutely will not stand for not having a school in the community. We'll have a private school somehow. It'll be a struggle, but if there's a will, there's a way."

It's not surprising, then, that residents didn't just embrace the eco-village idea; they committed to it wholeheartedly. The Craik Sustainable Living Project (CSLP) began with a document outlining a solidly constructed, meticulously detailed, and highly ambitious five-year plan to transform Craik into an energy-efficient, environmentally friendly community. Its vision statement read, in part: "The Town and the Rural Municipality of Craik… propose to embark on a joint, long-term project in search of ways of living that address the issue of sustainability and revitalization through physical demonstration of viable solutions…. We believe such an undertaking has tremendous potential for leading rural [Saskatchewan] into a new period of renewal and revitalization."

In other words, Craik was no longer interested in merely attracting more population; their goal was now to serve as a model of change for the entire province.

Dreams that big and statements that audacious often attract ridicule and disaster, but the townspeople spearheading the project knew how to insure against both. In addition to recognizing the community's tradition of tenacity and dedicated volunteerism, they knew that the key to success would lie in careful planning.

"No one knew much about eco-villages," says Shirley, "so we said, 'Before we start, let's build a demonstration building so it shows the community and the rural people that we're really serious.'"

The donated land was situated next to a golf course with grass greens that the rural municipality had recently built. "They needed a clubhouse," says Shirley. "That was the focal point. That got things going."

There were four facets to the five-year plan: construct the demonstration Eco-Centre; educate local residents and encourage them to adopt sustainable living practices; model ecologically sound principles for the rest of the province; and, finally, establish a representative eco-village of ten to twelve self-sustaining properties on the land next to the golf course. The plan included a number of socially and economically significant "green" initiatives, including attracting like-minded business, industry, and population to the area, establishing an annual Solar Fair to promote environmentally friendly practices, and building an eco-friendly marina at the regional park. In short, the Town and Rural Municipality of Craik planned to gradually but completely redefine itself over a specific time span.

Aaron Obrigewitsch was one of the first to volunteer his time and labour. He'd grown up in Craik, left for a few years, then returned. "I like small-town living," he says. "And I want to still have a small town to live in twenty and thirty years from now. This is a good place. We're fifty minutes from Moose Jaw. It's an hour and four minutes from my door to the Northgate Mall in Regina, and it's an hour and fourteen minutes from my door to Saskatoon. I drive 300 yards to go to work. My shop's in the middle of town and I live on the edge."

Aaron was a plumber by trade, but he soon found himself chairing the entire building committee, overseeing decisions far outside his comfort zone. "The learning curve for all of us was straight up," he says. "I knew nothing about solar panels or geothermal energy."

Lynn Oliphant, who lived in a straw bale house he'd built near Saskatoon, acted as advisor. As the demonstration Eco-Centre took shape, it must have been with a sense of wonder that participants came to appreciate just how much of the energy and materials they needed were right there under their feet, in the sky and on the land around them. The grand opening took place July 3, 2004. By then, word of the CSLP had spread.

The Eco-Centre and the grounds surrounding it were packed. "CBC's Lindy Thorsen came out and did his show from here," says Aaron. "CKTV was out. We did television interviews with CTV that day. It was a big, huge day."

The exposure was a small taste of what would come.

The Eco-Centre is a marvel of construction that is not only aesthetically beautiful but also almost totally clean-energy efficient. One end houses the golf course clubhouse, while the other consists of meeting rooms and the Solar Garden Restaurant, which specializes in cuisine using locally grown ingredients. There's also a lounge, and a gift shop that markets the fruits of the land and the talents of those living on it. Rainwater captured from the roof runs through a filtration system for appropriate domestic use. Grey water goes through a polishing process using broken, recycled glass before being circulated into the soil. A jacket on the chimney heats water. South-facing windows and rooftop solar panels pull in heat. Excess energy from the sun in the summer months is piped into the ground, supercharging the earth so heat pumps don't have to work so hard in the winter.

Duram wheat straw, baled by a local farmer, insulates the walls, and area farmers were only too happy to give up stones from their fields to decoratively cover a core inner wall of recycled cinderblock. Both the cinderblock and the stone retain and radiate heat, as does the large Finnish oven in the restaurant, a showpiece constructed from almost 3,000 bricks saved from the demolition of a local school in 1988.

"The chainlink fence came from an old fuel depot at Findlater," says Aaron. "There's a steel railing for the golf carts to park against, and I think that came from there also. The light standards are pipe that I had left over from a job." Interior beams and wood for the gorgeous double front doors were gleaned from demolished grain elevators in Craik and Maymont. The ceiling is solar-kiln-dried pine from another Saskatchewan community.

"There's as much recycled, reused stuff as possible," says Aaron. "Just about everything else came from the Habitat for Humanity ReStore in Saskatoon."

"But things have to work," he points out. The lights on

the gas line standards are new, as are the indoor sinks and faucets. "This is a public building. You can't have a water pump to wash your hands because the health inspector won't allow that type of thing."

Indeed, the building appears clean and modern in every way, right down to the composting toilets, which no one would differentiate from regular toilets were it not for the signs. Natural light pours through the windows, green vines twist and trail around magnificent beams and the aroma of fresh bread emanates from the stunning masonry oven.

Best of all, the centre is busy, which means it's creating environmental awareness and generating revenue at the same time. It's become a popular spot for area residents to meet, dine, and/or play a round of golf. It also operates as a facility from which to run seminars and workshops on the environment. Roughly equidistant from Moose Jaw, Regina, and Saskatoon it has proven a convenient location for outside organizations to host meetings and conferences, environment-related or otherwise.

Due to the nature of the project and the attitude of goodwill characteristic of many small towns, some opportunities for income weren't immediately recognized. While the building was still under construction, curiosity-seekers appeared. At first, whoever was working would lay down their hammer and oblige them with a tour. "Part of the whole project is education," says Aaron, "so when people are interested enough to come out and take a look, we want to make sure we show them." Tour groups ranged in size from two to sixty, and cropped up every other day or so.

With each tour taking up to an hour and a half, the task became time-consuming.

"The trouble is, we all have jobs," says Aaron. "Most things are run on volunteers, whether at the park, the rink, the Eco-Centre or wherever." Aaron spends the equivalent of two days each week working for free, but he looks to others to illustrate his point. "The golf course manager worked at the Eco-Centre every day for almost two months. That was no pay, just work. He gives tours too. He'll be an hour and a half and then he'll end up working until seven to finish what he has to do."

Eventually the tour guides mobilized and organized. "We started a company called Pelican Eco-tours and charge five dollars a person. We didn't want to charge, but honestly, we all work."

Pelican Eco-tours is now a valued source of revenue. Other funding comes from various community endeavours (including raffling fuel-efficient vehicles, such as the "smart car"), and private, corporate, and government sponsorship and contributions.

Volunteer labour is monumental. "Hundreds have been involved," says Aaron. "We've had people from just about all over Canada working on the building. They'll read about it on the website and come and spend a day or two, helping to put up bales, or whatever."

But running the Eco-Centre hasn't always been smooth or easy. Promised money has failed to appear after changes in government posts or policies. Grants are available for environment-related projects, but they must be ferreted out. Organizations want assurances that a project will be successful before committing the dollars necessary to make it so. Money has come in dribs and drabs, but the Town and Municipality have persisted, and as the integrity of the project has become well known, purse strings have loosened.

As the demonstration Eco-Centre was going up other facets of the five-year plan got underway. Through workshops and seminars area residents learned about conservation, recycling, renewable energy, global warming, growing your own food, and composting.

"We're trying to hammer home to people that sustainable living means shopping at home too," Shirley explains. "You're always going to have people who think the city is better, and in some cases it is, but we keep trying."

It was a campaign of education, not coercion, yet a few locals resisted—invariably older residents who neither wanted nor needed change. "They're not looking fifty years into the future," says Aaron. "They see us spending all this money on the centre that we could be spending in town to keep services, probably until they're gone. But I'm convinced that we have to do this project to have a town in ten years. If we just hunker down and close the borders, within ten years we're going to be a town with no business—maybe a coffee shop and a bar. I don't want that. We have to do this to ensure our long-term survival."

Inevitably, coffee-shop talk fostered misunderstandings. "They're not doing it on purpose," says Aaron. "They say a lot of stuff I'm sure they think is true, but it's not. So we spend a lot of time trying to make sure everybody knows what's really happening." He smiles as he relates how people are changing in spite of themselves. "They go to the lumber yard and buy soaker hoses instead of big sprinklers. These are the people who are against the project. They don't even realize it, but they're thinking more that way." Shirley notes other subtle shifts in thinking. Naysayers are now proud of the completed demonstration building, preferring to take ownership of the success rather than deride it.

To model responsible environmental management, the town and municipality took the initiative in gradually retrofitting existing buildings and using recycled materials for maintenance, like roofing made from tires.

The project has also assembled an ongoing assortment of print and resource material designed for public use. Today it consists of more than 200 items in a special collection at the Craik Public Library. As well, Climate Change Awareness and Action, a course targeting elementary and middle school students, was developed and officially piloted in the Craik School in 2006. The course, the first of its kind in Saskatchewan, is on track for incorporation into curriculums province-wide.

A seminar series for adults on sustainable living alternatives is complemented by opportunities to stimulate the economy through job and revenue creation, with an emphasis on finding sustainable ways to grow and market products that until now have been produced conventionally and purchased outside the area. Before the Eco-Centre was complete, these seminars were held in the community hall. According to Shirley, initial turnout was "18 people or so" but has been growing ever since.

For a community that was defining and promoting itself exclusively as environmentally aware and responsible, the golf course, completed just before the idea was pitched, was a conundrum. "A lot of people comment that a golf course and a sustainable living project don't mesh very well," says Aaron. "The word 'environment' was never mentioned when they built it. We just tried to tie it in and swallow it up somehow."

However, the committee hadn't counted on the resourcefulness of the course manager, who tackled with gusto the job of aligning the course with the new theme. "He composts all the grass clippings and uses very little fertilizer," says Aaron. "He's very select about it and he's got a strict watering regimen that uses probably half the water of most courses." Yet the fairways are as green as any on the prairies. The golf course had originally been proposed as a draw to help boost the local economy, a plan that had succeeded in many other rural communities. "We were working and working to try to get it nicer and get it busier and advertise and get more people out," laughs Aaron. "Last weekend I couldn't get a tee-time until 4:45. I guess we've succeeded."

Adjacent to the golf course, at the other end of the building, display gardens showcase approximately 300 species of plants that thrive under drought-like prairie conditions. The gardens not only beautify the area, but also demonstrate sustainable landscaping methods such as xeriscaping and site reclamation. Stands of trees have also been planted.

They act as shelter belts and noise barriers, provide habitat for wildlife, purify the air and, like everything else in the demonstration community, serve as an educational tool.

The shelter groves, representing fifty-five species of trees, are a buffer between the Louis Riel Trail (Highway 11) and the CSLP's most ambitious objective: the eco-village. While through all these initiatives Craik was slowly transitioning into a model of environmental stewardship, the eco-village was evolving. On the 127 acres donated by the municipality, a road was built, lots surveyed and land sub-divided. Interested parties were required to submit building plans for energy-efficient, sustainable housing. Buyers could acquire a lot for one dollar, with the option of leasing an additional five acres of land from the rural municipality for ecologically sound income-generating purposes (market gardens, greenhouses, and the like).

The mayor of Craik sold his house and purchased the first lot.

For all their outward enthusiasm, organizers did feel some skepticism about the plan. Building the Eco-Centre provided a burst of growth to the economy, but in order to maintain it, people from outside the community had to buy into the sustainability concept and move to Craik to live out the dream. In 2004, Aaron said he'd be happy to see just three lots sold. After all, Craik had pinned its future hopes on just two more families moving in. But by the end of 2007, all nine available lots had sold. Landowners were already established on some, and others were in the process of development. By 2009, interest was so great that the rural municipality began surveying more lots for a phase two expansion.

In less than a decade, the face of Craik and district has changed dramatically. People from across the continent and beyond have heard about what's taking place there. An international school is under construction; when it is completed, it will teach English as a second language, first to people from Korea, as well as environmental stewardship and sustainable living practices to hundreds of future students.

In addition to occupation of the eco-village, new life is sparking within the town as well. People interested in a back-to-the-land existence are buying properties and moving to the community they know supports their views. They're making a living there and putting their dollars back into the local economy. "Green" business and industry is taking a serious look at the area.

But there continue to be stumbling blocks. A multi-million-dollar fibre mill years in the planning fell through at the eleventh hour when provincial and federal support failed. Recently, however, Titan Clean Energy Projects Corporation purchased land to set up shop producing energy products from organic waste for markets across North America. It also runs a composting program in the community and plays a role in researching future clean energy options. As well, Golden Flax 4 U Inc. erected a 2,100-square-foot building of flax straw bales to promote the many uses of flax and sell the numerous products generated from it (straw building-bales, soap, seeds, etc.). In a win-win arrangement, area farmers are producing crops they can market locally to support such endeavours.

It seems there are as many opportunities in Craik as there are people. "There are a billion things we want to do," says Aaron. "It just takes one person to say, 'I'm going to do this,' and take it by the horns." He cites a CSLP brand on locally grown organic grain products as one example. Many more ideas have emerged from the Sustainable Rural Alternatives Seminar Series.

The five-year plan ended in April of 2008, but momentum was only beginning. Of the twenty-four specific goals laid out in the plan, twenty-three have been met or exceeded. All that remains of the original objectives is a marina.

"The Friendliest Place by a Dam Site" has morphed into "The Environmentally Friendliest Place by a Dam Site." The success of the Craik Sustainable Living Project defies imagination. Due to the vision and commitment of citizens and volunteers, the project and the people involved with it have won numerous awards and received substantial national and international recognition.

"By promoting environmental sustainability we thought we could bring people to town," says Aaron. "We had no idea what we were getting into." The population of the town has increased from 418 in 2001 to 450 in 2009. With further expansion taking place, survival is no longer an issue.

The air in Craik and district hums with excitement. People who visit get caught up in the spirit of wanting to get involved. In a world accustomed to turning on the news to messages of war, crime and natural disaster, there is a hunger to be part of something good. People in Craik feel good about themselves. Just like Superman, they know they're impacting the world in positive ways. And they're happy.

Chapter 6
Meacham

Herbert Has Lots For A Buck   Elizabeth McLachlan

Meacham

Illusion vs. Reality

The village of Meacham, tucked off a bend in the #2 highway approximately sixty kilometres east of Saskatoon, Saskatchewan, is reminiscent of a delightful magician's trick. It is not what it appears to be. Meacham is a slip of a village with a population of seventy. It lies off the beaten track, yet hundreds regularly beat a path to its doors. Upon arrival, they find a community that appears on the verge of disintegration. Prairie grass encroaches upon unpaved streets, races unimpeded across empty lots, insinuates itself around weathered, abandoned buildings, and materializes over the scars left from ripped-out rails. The name of the grain company on the lone remaining elevator is obliterated, signifying desertion of a town that once possessed five of the pillars of progress. Main Street consists only of a decades-old hotel and bar, a village office, and a credit union. Tubs of flowers, modern upgrades to the office, and the presence of recycling bins are the first clues that life exists here at all.

In its heyday, Meacham was a buzzing farming community of several hundred people. However, as trends towards larger farms and smaller families strengthened, the town began to fade. Gradually schools, churches, shops, and medical services disappeared, as did children, who grew up and moved away. No new families arrived to take their place. There was nothing to lure them. Longtime residents sadly watched as establishments closed and buildings were abandoned, demolished, or moved out of town. Like sand coursing through fingers, their town was slipping away.

Revitalization arrived unexpectedly. In 1979, Charley Farrero, a sculptor, and his wife June Jacobs, a fibre artist, were looking for a place to live and establish studios. They knew people in Meacham, notably fellow artist Greg Hardy, and decided to buy property there.

"Meacham was close enough to an urban community to hopefully draw customers," says June. "Close enough to potentially get product to market, but far enough away and inexpensive enough to have a residence and a place to work that fits within that bottom category of income where most artists are situated."

Charley set up his studio in a small building in the village and June opened a craft shop at the nearby junction of Highways 5 and 2. Within two years, artist friend Anita Rocamora followed. She was seeking affordable accommodation, the company of colleagues, and a good place to raise her daughter.

The appearance of professional artists in their community came as a surprise to the people of Meacham, but June points out that where you find one artist, you'll likely find others. She, Charley, Greg, and Anita formed a small nucleus towards which fellow aesthetes gravitated. As they arrived, they purchased property for homes and studios, enlivened formerly vacant buildings, and added population to the village. Jewellers, weavers, painters, sculptors, musicians, papermakers, and even a composer who set up a recording studio all came to Meacham. Many moved there permanently, while others established studios in the town but lived in nearby Saskatoon. Some—like a Toronto-based television art director—bought summer homes.

"In order for a community to survive, you need people paying taxes," says June. "Here you have artists paying taxes by simply occupying places. They also pay taxes on property they own. It benefits the whole community because these buildings could be empty or moved away."

In 1986, Greg Hardy sold June and Charley his tiny house so that he could split his time between a nearby farm and the city of Saskatoon, and June moved her busy little shop into the village. She named it the Hand Wave Gallery and designed a logo. The clenched fist trying to contain the slipping sand became an open hand on signs and banners beckoning people into Meacham.

Longtime residents, however, weren't so ready to extend that welcoming hand. They were never hostile towards the newcomers, but fear and lack of understanding made them cautious.

"The arts don't always have a good reputation," says June. The perception that artists are free-spirited bohemians was difficult to overcome, in large part because of their working hours. "You don't go off to a job like other people do," she says, "like a schoolteacher, a potash worker doing shift work or a farmer doing seasonal work. You work when you work. Sometimes it might be all night long because you're into something. Your weekend may be in the middle of the week or you may be working on a series of things and then you're exhausted by it, so you won't be working at all. It took a while for people to understand that yes, artists do pay their taxes. They cut their grass and plant their gardens. They have children who go to school. They are normal."

Few of June's new neighbours, for instance, knew that she had grown up on a farm, was trained as a home economist, and had worked in that capacity for a utility company for years. Before they discovered Meacham, she and Charley had been looking for a farmyard. "Fear keeps some more distant that it should," she says. She speaks for artists in general when she states, "We're very accessible and we're not really any different."

Even if residents did not understand the lifestyle or the work of the artists in their midst, they did grasp the significance of their success. As Charley and others became internationally recognized a sense of pride developed. The Hand Wave Gallery, which showcases the work of seventy-five Saskatchewan artisans, became a favourite place to bring out-of-town guests.

For their part, the artists engaged with the community in typical ways. "We got involved when we thought our interests would coincide," says June. "I was a school trustee for eleven years, and Charley was on the volunteer fire department." As their children grew, the couple helped with baseball, soccer, and the summer games. They continue to support activities locally and in the surrounding communities.

Over time, Charley further proved his affinity with the people of Meacham by saving significant buildings. When he needed a larger studio, he bought a former fabric store that was sitting empty. "It has history," says June. "In the early 1970s people travelled from all over to buy yardage. Then the business terminated." The building held sentimental value for many who were pleased to see it in use again. He also acquired the 1949 schoolhouse. Such actions helped dispel any lingering notion that outsiders could never integrate into the community.

Another building in danger of being lost was the Ukrainian Hall. So dear was this structure to town residents that when it went up for sale they could hardly bear the thought that it might be hauled out of town to house livestock. Fortunately something much better was in store.

Angus and Louisa Ferguson had no idea that Meacham was home to a thriving artistic community when they chose to move there in the early 1990s. They simply wanted a quiet, bucolic lifestyle within commuting distance of Saskatoon. The couple was heavily into live theatre and dreamed of establishing a professional company on the prairie. With this in mind, they bought the schoolhouse from Charley.

It was big enough for both living quarters and performance space.

However, the arrival of children stalled their theatre plans and filled the extra space, and by the time they were ready to proceed, the much better venue of the Ukrainian Hall presented itself. The 1925 building already had a stage, and since its original décor had rarely been updated, it was loaded with character.

Angus and Louisa refinanced their schoolhouse home and purchased the hall for five thousand dollars. But the venture wasn't solid enough for bankers to willingly back it. Only on the strength of donations and a handful of investors could renovations commence.

Harvest Hall was to be a venue not just for plays, but for concerts, workshops, literary readings, and all manner of culturally enriching pursuits. From the outset the Fergusons were anxious to include the community. They maintained an open door policy for everything, from renovations to rehearsals. Anyone was welcome to drop in. Some members of the public brought tools and pitched in. The first official event, in September 1997, was a drumming workshop. The opening play in November, *Billy Bishop Goes to War,* highlighted a Canadian war hero, and the first Christmas reinforced a family theme, with sleigh rides, a bonfire, traditional pantomime, and performers mingling and eating with the audience. As much as possible, Canada, community, and theatre are juxtaposed.

Today Dancing Sky Theatre is the consummate expression of Meacham's focal evolution from agriculture to the arts. More than the merging of humour and pathos symbolized by the comedy and tragedy masks of live theatre, it represents the melding of opposing elements: rural and urban, amateur and professional, contemporary and classic, past and future. The historical integrity of the building is preserved despite its novel new purpose. Production schedules are designed to work within the rhythm of farm life. The professional theatre is often a launching point for up-and-coming actors. They perform the classics, but there is also a major focus on drama that reflects local and rural issues. Since these plays are hard to come by, Dancing Sky Theatre regularly commissions work from Saskatchewan and Canadian playwrights. In 2005, however, there came a delightful twist when they themselves were commissioned to create a play for Saskatchewan's centennial. The urbanity of professional theatre takes on rural flavour as it provides food for the body and for the soul. While everyone is welcome, there is an emphasis on employing Saskatchewan actors and attracting audiences from small surrounding communities. Theatregoers travel 100 kilometres or more and can have dinner before the performance. The menu features ingredients from Saskatchewan producers whenever possible.

Dancing Sky Theatre was an immediate success. That first performance opened with applause and closed to a standing ovation. Plays are now often sold out before opening night. That the community supported it as their own from the beginning is testament to their acceptance of artists, and the arts, as a defining characteristic of the town.

The agricultural component of Meacham continues to wane. Recently a well-established farm implement dealer was forced to close. "As I understand it, suppliers wanted a bigger centre," says Betty Saretzsky, longtime village clerk who has recently retired. At the same time, the cultural component waxes. Size clearly doesn't matter to the artists who choose Meacham as their base from which to pursue their muse. Nor does it matter to the multitudes who flock there to enjoy the results. A quick scan of media releases reveals a distinct jump in the buzz surrounding the village since the theatre opened. A new venture, Harvest Moon Antiques, Gifts and Gallery opened in 2008, with a café to follow a year later. Creative people continue to move to Meacham, some on the strength of reading about the place. They come, they pay taxes, they draw in a customer base and they raise Meacham's profile on the map. They are now the core of the community. Fear and resistance has evolved into support and pride, made tangible by the addition of the word "culture" to "agriculture," "industry," and "business" on the town sign.

Cultural refinement has traditionally been associated with urban environments. The airs of urban affectation, however, are nowhere to be found in Meacham. Just as Shakespeare wrote his plays for the masses, Dancing Sky brings theatre to ordinary people, and artists and artisans merge with and emerge from the place and its people. In the town's profitable hotel bar, country and western music and a contemporary art installation are equally at home.

A Shakespearean actor coming to Meacham wouldn't

be far wrong in applying Macbeth's observation "nothing is but what is not" to the little town. Meacham is not what it appears to be—an obscure little pocket of people fading quietly into quack grass and dust. Rather it is a hive of industrious creativity, well-placed for future survival.

Chapter 7
Plum Coulee

Plum Coulee

Teetotalling and Tippling: No Great Divide

People of diverse faiths, backgrounds, and ethnicities coming together to grow a town is not extraordinary—but what's happening in Plum Coulee, Manitoba, a community of 770 people located seventeen kilometres southwest of Winnipeg, is an impressive case of two seemingly incompatible groups working hand in hand: a community of Mennonites, who typically disapprove of drinking and the hazardous consequences it can wreak, and a pioneer family whose significant fortune and philanthropic activities are made possible by the manufacture and sale of alcohol.

In the mid-1880s, a Canadian Pacific Railway labourer scratched a line across southern Manitoba with a single, horse-drawn blade. Behind him followed section men with ties, rails, and spikes. More than a decade earlier, surveyors had staked their route, marking and labeling the vast, virgin territory from which would eventually rise towns they could only imagine. As they plodded mile after endless mile, farther and farther from supplies and civilization, the spectre of mounting privation must surely have haunted them. Perhaps this is why they were so delighted when, in 1872, one particular coulee yielded an unexpected treasure along its creek banks: a multitude of wild plum trees adorned with scores of jewel-like plums within easy plucking reach. Enjoying the extravagance of the succulent fruit, it was easy to name the place that soon disappeared in the dust of their retreating boots—Plum Coulee.

The new railroad brought to the coulee settlers of many nationalities: Austrian, Russian, Scottish, English, Irish, and Jewish, to name a few. Regardless of origin, everyone who came was starting from scratch—new settlers in a new country breaking new land, establishing new businesses and creating a common history. They took each other at face value and saw one another as equals. Hard work and community-mindedness were what counted.

Religious and ethnic differences were more than tolerated; they were respected. Businesses, schools, and churches cooperated together to ensure everyone's interests were met. Differing denominations held joint services or shared available buildings for worship. And when the Baptists built a church, they allowed other faiths to use it.

Mennonite farms and street villages rose up in the surrounding area. Their residents came to Plum Coulee to engage in commerce, further strengthening cross-cultural ties. By 1893, several Mennonites had moved into the village and started businesses, some with non-Mennonite partners. Their horticultural and business acumen contributed to the success of the community which, by 1897, was well on its way, with seven grain elevators and two flour mills.

Plum Coulee was incorporated as a village in 1901. By 1907, a significant contingent of Jewish settlers added to the mix of pioneering souls. Two of them, the village storekeeper's daughter and a humble woodcutter living nearby, had no way of knowing their actions would be instrumental in ensuring the community's survival a century later.

As the great railroad continued to press west, and more and more opportunities for settlement opened, adventure beckoned. Many Plum Coulee residents answered the call. Most had arrived in Canada alone or with their families, and it was easy to pull up stakes and move westward. Mennonites also ventured forth as they became more and more acculturated to Canadian ways. But since they had migrated in large groups, they were not inclined to disperse. Instead they left street villages and farms and filtered into nearby towns. In this manner, the composition of Plum Coulee, while remaining multi-ethnic, gradually became primarily Mennonite.

Plum Coulee was a strong little community. Nevertheless, it took a century after its incorporation as a village to achieve town status. By then, in 2001, Canadian settlement patterns had undergone an about-face. The push to populate rural Canada had become the drive to depopulate it. Small communities dried up as services moved to urban areas and people followed them. In Plum Coulee, a general spiral downward had brought many losses, including the disappearance of all but two of its original seven grain elevators. Residents knew their community's continuing survival was tenuous.

One of the first questions that citizens of a threatened community ask is, "What makes our town memorable? What is our claim to fame?" Sadly, the answer for Plum Coulee was Bloody Jack.

John Larry Krafchenko was a bright seven-year-old when he emigrated with his parents from Romania in 1888. A pleasant, model child at home, no one could ever determine why he developed such a maniacal problem with authority. His first known encounter with the law took place at the age of eleven, when he stole several watches from a store. At fifteen, he was jailed for bicycle theft. What ensued was a confusing and escalating pattern of good and evil behaviour, marked by both crime and extraordinary compassion. Krafchenko's school attendance was spotty, yet he managed to become fluent in at least five languages and could easily fool others into believing he was well-educated and upstanding. More than once, he successfully impersonated a doctor and a teacher. He channeled his capacity for startling, uncontrollable fits of rage into a career as a professional wrestler. When he left that profession, an apparent change of heart led him to the lecture circuit to expound upon the virtues of temperance—however, he was also operating a side business passing fraudulent cheques.

Despite Krafchenko's seeming lack of moral conscience, he was eminently charming and dangerously handsome. Many a good man and woman committed deeds they would ordinarily never have considered were it not for Krafchenko's charisma. Strangely, as his life of crime deepened, so did his acts of compassion. Writing bad cheques with a pen evolved into robbing banks with a gun, and staging daring jailbreaks. Yet on several occasions he allowed himself to be captured rather than use his firearm, which was loaded and within reach. As a fugitive he once came out of hiding to testify on a friend's behalf, knowing it would mean his own recapture and incarceration.

Krafchenko must have been a homebody at heart, for despite his global travels, which included stints wrestling in Australia and the United States, bankrobbing sprees in England, Germany, Italy and the United States, and a sojourn in Russia where he found a wife, he consistently gravitated back to the Plum Coulee area. His charm and his luck ran out there, when he decided to rob the local Bank of Montreal. In the process, he shot and killed the manager. Before Krafchenko was hanged for the murder, he pled innocence, but there were enough local witnesses to convince the judge of his guilt. One of them was the liveryman whose vehicle and driving services Krafchenko commandeered for the getaway. Strangely, though he knew the man had witnessed the murder, Krafchenko let him go free, admonishing him only to cook up a convincing fiction to explain his whereabouts at the time of the robbery.

The wild life of this Plum Coulee pioneer was certainly

a memorable part of the town's history, but it's easy to understand why residents didn't care to capitalize on it as a tool to renew their town.

However, Plum Coulee boasted another citizen of note: Saidye Rosner, whose Jewish father was a founding member and onetime mayor of the town. He owned the general store across from the burgled bank and, ironically, had tried to steer Krafchenko from his wayward ways. Like Krafchenko, Saidye too was smart and compassionate, but she put her attributes to good use. Well before she reached adulthood, she served as president of the Girls' Auxiliary of the Western Jewish Orphans' Home. She married Samuel Bronfman, son of Mindel and Yechiel Bronfman who, like the Rosners, had fled Czarist Russia in the 1890s and, after a brief stay in Saskatchewan, came to Manitoba as refugees. Yechiel had made a fortune as a tobacco farmer in Russia. It was a letdown to discover that the Canadian climate prohibited him from repeating that success. The formerly affluent businessman went to work as a labourer on the railroad and later in a sawmill. Yechiel taught his sons that fortunes were made on hard work and ingenuity, and together they were constantly on the lookout for business opportunities. Working in a sawmill led to selling firewood. Soon they were selling frozen whitefish as well and earning a good living. Horses were in high demand, and Yechiel's business sense next led them into horse trading. Through doing business in hotels and bars, the ever-observant Bronfmans recognized huge potential in the hospitality industry. By the time they bought a hotel, in 1903, Yechiel and sons were well on their way to earning a new fortune.

As he got to know the hotel trade, one son, Samuel, noted that the real money was in liquor sales. Having learned well from his father, he leapt at the opportunity to establish himself as a distributor. Perhaps it is significant that in Yiddish the name Bronfman means "liquor man," for he went on to become fabulously wealthy, organizing a distiller's corporation in Montreal and eventually buying out Joseph E. Seagram & Sons, whose popular brands became even more famous in Samuel's capable hands. Of course, timing helped. During the 1920s the manufacture and sale of alcohol was strictly prohibited in the United States, making the "devil water" that much more desirable to imbibers. Men the likes of Al Capone went to legendary lengths to ensure it was available, and in the process engaged in crimes far more heinous than intoxication. Since Prohibition was not strictly in effect across Canada, however, Samuel was able to legally distil the stuff and make a fortune selling it to parched patrons from the States.

Although Samuel was acquainted with Al Capone, and his livelihood kept him dangerously close to the edge, he was essentially a man of integrity who was careful to live within the law. In 1922 he married a woman of similar proclivity—the Plum Coulee storekeeper's daughter. True to their natures, the couple was aware of their great good fortune and planned to share it. By 1952, they were wealthy enough to found the Samuel and Saidye Bronfman Family Foundation and become one of the richest, best-known philanthropic families in Canada. Their generosity was so broad and open-hearted that they made a point of supporting McGill University despite its reputation at the time as a hotbed of anti-Semitism. The Bronfmans' ongoing contributions of money and assets to the university resulted in greatly mitigating the taint on its name.

Samuel and Saidye worked tirelessly for Jewish causes, and they supported many other efforts as well. Saidye in particular was a much-loved patron of the arts. The couple instilled in their four children the importance of hard work, education, and the desire to make a better world.

The saga of Bloody Jack and the success of the Bronfmans were two of the histories that came to light as Plum Coulee residents worked on a centennial history book. For some, it must have seemed a requiem to a lost era. The town had changed. Heather Unger, chair of the Plum Coulee Community Foundation, points out that the disappearance of local businesses and lower local employment levels were changing Plum Coulee from a farming community into a bedroom community. "Downtown was dying, along with community spirit," she says. If ever the time was right to revive the Plum Coulee of the past, it was now.

A bevy of volunteers contacted past citizens and researched family histories for the book. Of course, the Rosner family was included. Saidye's husband Samuel had passed away in 1971, thirty years earlier, but by happy circumstance their daughter, Phyllis Lambert, attended the centennial celebrations. Phyllis was a successful career woman who had distinguished herself in architecture. Her lengthy list of accomplishments included founding the world-class Canadian Centre for Architecture and being named to the Order of Canada. She took a keen interest in Plum Coulee, the place her mother was raised and from which her own roots grew.

Phyllis' enthusiasm inspired hope. "The visit sparked interest in the Bronfman family," says Heather. "A local gal came across the Samuel and Saidye Bronfman Family Foundation website, and conversations started as to what might be possible with their support."

The people of Plum Coulee knew they'd lost something special about their town, and they wanted to bring it back. Renewed well-being would draw people and fresh energy. In days gone by the downtown core was the hub of the community. Folk of every faith and walk of life gathered in the central square to visit, enjoy concerts, shop, and attend town meetings. The square was still there, but it had fallen into disuse. Downtown was still there too, but like the square, it was a shadow of its former self. Even the plum trees that had brought a name and such beauty to the village were diminishing. In 2001, the closure of the Agricore United grain elevator, one of the only two left standing, was another blow. However, if the town square, the plum trees and the elevator could be resurrected, and perhaps used in new ways, the town might come alive once more. The infrastructure and the ideas were there; the resources weren't.

So the Bronfman family was approached. Phyllis Lambert's architectural eye sparkled at the prospect of restoring Plum Coulee on a grand scale. Why stop with just the downtown core? She put the town in touch with the Winnipeg firm of Hilderman Thomas Frank Cram Landscape Architecture and Planning. Garry Hilderman himself took the project under his wing. With experts in planning and design at their disposal, and an eight-year funding partnership with the Bronfman Family Foundation in place, a world of possibilities opened to the community. Plum Coulee began to imagine what had formerly been inconceivable. Within a year of what some feared would be their last centennial, the town had struck a five-year Master Plan to restore and revitalize the entire community. Two committees were created: the Plum Coulee Community Foundation, which administers the funds and raises matching contributions in support of community projects in general, and the Heritage Recreation Development Corporation, which oversees completion of the Master Plan.

For 725 people to take on the task of overhauling the entire town was heady stuff, but with architects and financial resources secured, it didn't take long for the old town spirit to fire once more. All that was needed was determination and a lot of volunteers.

The main premise of the plan was to work with what the town already had in order to recreate and enhance its former vibrancy. The town lobbied Agricore United to acquire the decommissioned elevator. It was only twenty-six years old, young for a wooden grain elevator, and still in excellent shape. The effort was successful. "One dollar was paid to Agricore by the town for the purchase," says Heather.

The Winnipeg architects drew up exciting long-range plans for the 110-foot-tall structure, including shops, office space, a seniors' centre, and a daycare. Something for everyone. To top it off, an upper-level restaurant overlooking the prairie would provide a spectacular view. Development of the Prairie View Elevator got underway in 2004. "Currently it has a new roof, [and] some renovations to the office space and restrooms were built," says Heather. It is also an interpretive centre offering ongoing tours, and it is home to the Plum Coulee Community Foundation office.

Other projects are just as exciting. Wild plum trees, the town's namesake, have been re-vegetated en masse. Many along Main Avenue were donated and bear plaques relating compelling snippets of Plum Coulee history. Flower beds grace every corner, and old-fashioned street lamps line the Avenue. Where unattractive sidewalks once crumbled, brick walkways now draw strollers to quaintly refurbished storefronts and businesses with unique names like Daisy Cakes Café and Loon Magic Gallery.

Heritage Square, the hotspot of bygone days, has been revived with a park, complete with a fountain, more flower beds and a themed picnic shelter in which Plum Coulee's railroad history is highlighted. The old town bell guards one end of the square and an open-air skating rink the other. In summer the iceless surface serves for other sports.

Outdoorism has always been popular in Plum Coulee. Imagine a town with a beach in its centre. Just such a thing was developed off Main Avenue when the old reservoir was drained and resurrected as a swimming hole, complete with sandy beach, docks, and sun shelters. Fringed with hundreds of newly planted trees, Sunset Beach is now a popular leisure destination for locals and visitors of every age.

In addition, a system of well-maintained paths loops along Plum River and through Plum Coulee's many green spaces, carrying cyclists, hikers, snowmobilers, and cross-country skiers across scenic vistas, either past town into the sweeping prairie or in the other direction, where Heritage Square, churches, schools, the museum and an art gallery form the heart of the community.

The Plum Coulee revitalization was so successful that by the summer of 2006 the planned Centennial Park campground facility was a welcome addition. Expansion into even more campsites took place the following year.

The beauty of Plum Coulee's Heritage and Recreation Master Plan was always to benefit local residents and draw out-of-towners. This it has, but tourism alone rarely keeps a town alive. Plum Coulee is always looking for economical, innovative ways to better the town. In 2009 it won an Association of Manitoba Municipalities Award with nearby Altona for demonstrating initiative and creativity in combining police forces to share costs and resources.

Concurrently with implementing the Heritage and Recreation Master Plan, the town also worked to acquire and zone a significant amount of land for new industry, commercial enterprises and residences. New home builders are offered impressive tax incentives. A 100 per cent rebate on town property taxes the first year of occupancy, a 50 per cent rebate the second year, and 25 per cent in the third are enticing attractions.

These perks, along with Plum Coulee's restoration

project and its reputation for forward thinking and cross-cultural appreciation, are working. The population rose from 725 to 770 in five years. In 2004 the community caught the attention of the Mennonite Central Committee (MCC), a worldwide Anabaptist ministry devoted to disaster relief, sustainable community development, and other peace and justice efforts. It chose Plum Coulee as the home of its Canadian national warehouse. The massive 7,200-square-foot facility is a central clearing house for the distribution of emergency supplies. Other warehouses in Canada ship these items to Plum Coulee, where they are organized and bundled by volunteers to send to troubled zones throughout the world. Because the MCC relies so heavily on volunteers, they knew Plum Coulee was the right location for this facility. Hundreds from the many Mennonite communities surrounding the town come to Plum Coulee to give of their time. It's a win-win situation. The MCC operates a thriving warehouse due to the strong Plum Coulee and area volunteer base, and Plum Coulee benefits from the high profile the national warehouse gives it.

Saidye Rosner Bronfman would have loved the new town. Volunteerism defined her life from the time she spent as a young girl working with orphans, through the Second World War, when her efforts earned her the title of Officer of the Order of the British Empire, and well on into her nineties. Before she became wealthy she volunteered her time; later she gave both time and money. Her obituary in the July 7, 1995 *Globe and Mail* stated, "Mrs. Bronfman said the real credit must go to volunteers, not philanthropists."

The story included a familiar Saidye quote: "True leadership lies in volunteer commitment and energy."

Her daughter would agree. "Phyllis visits annually," says Heather. "She has a great deal of knowledge that she shares and is a wonderful motivator to our volunteers."

The Town of Plum Coulee website states, "Plum Coulee has a history of people working together to build a stronger community." A 2005 version elaborated the point. "Lutherans, Baptists, Jews, Catholics and Mennonites co-existed and respected each other's beliefs at a time when this was unheard of in other parts of the world."

The biblical admonishment not to judge lest you be judged was taken to heart by both current and former residents of Plum Coulee, with amazing results. All came together to revive the town. And in a respectful, equal partnership, two factions that might have been at odds in a different time and place—the Jewish Bronfmans, who made their fortune in alcohol, and Christian Mennonites who advocate sobriety—worked together to save their town.

Postscript: A few months after this chapter was written, Heather Unger sent me an update.

"Daisy Cakes has been sold," she said, *"and the three local sisters who run it have changed the name to Anna Joe's Bistro. The old main avenue museum has been moved into the grain elevator. Our new housing development sold out of lots, and a new developer has put in streets and services for another on the north side of town. Our population has snuck up to just*

over 800, which is putting space pressure on our K-8 school to expand with classroom additions. All is well in bedroom-community living in 2012."

Indeed.

Chapter 8
Vulcan

Vulcan

To Live Long and Prosper

When in 1910 a prairie village built around wheat names itself after the god of fire and dubs its streets Apollo, Jupiter, Neptune, and such like, you know imagination abounds. Eventually cooler heads prevailed, and Vulcan, halfway between the cities of Calgary and Lethbridge in southern Alberta, changed its street names to numbers. But in 1998 they were all changed back again. The community's collective imagination had fired once more.

It all started in 1964, when American Gene Roddenberry successfully marketed a television program he described as "*Wagon Train* in space"—the science fiction equivalent to stories about taming the Wild West. The series *Star Trek* was cancelled after only three seasons, but the shaky beginning was enough to make it memorable to viewers across North

America, especially after the series was sold into syndication. One particularly notable character was Spock, from the fictional planet Vulcan. A distinguishing feature of Spock's species was large ears that taper up to a pronounced point. In the very real community of Vulcan, Alberta the story goes that kids on local sports teams were subjected by their rivals to jibes, jeers and jests about the size of their ears. It was all taken in humourous stride. And when strangers started showing up in town to have their pictures taken displaying the "live long and prosper" gesture (a "planet Vulcan" four-fingered variation of the familiar peace sign of the sixties), town residents were further amused.

By the mid-1980s the community was failing. Once an agricultural giant with its famous "nine-in-a-line" row of grain elevators rising from the heart of the wheat belt, Vulcan was slowly succumbing to urbanization's tightening chokehold on rural economies. Like many small towns in decline, it was gasping for a way to survive.

Star Trek: The Motion Picture had by then found box office success, and numerous movie sequels, a second television series, and a string of books had propelled the story and its characters to cult phenomenon status. In Vulcan, Alberta the significance of the *Star Trek* connection couldn't be denied. An opportunity to rebrand the town with a science-fiction space travel theme geared to the series was obvious. Such a focus had the potential to draw large numbers of tourists and boost the flagging economy. But for a quiet prairie community that for generations had been associated with agriculture to suddenly identify itself with aliens from a fictional planet was an astronomical risk. It wasn't just a question of "what would the neighbours think?"—it was a question of whether the plan would even work. The mission of the series' Starship *Enterprise* to "boldly go where no man has gone before" was never truer than for this town of 1,400.

Fortunately, the people of Vulcan were more than zany enough to pull off the venture. There was skepticism, yes, but the level of full-out opposition was milder than expected, and the town's notorious sense of humour and imagination won out. Organizer Greg Dietz's comment to the *Edmonton Journal* in 1993 sums up the attitude of Vulcan residents in general: "It's good clean fun and it doesn't hurt anyone." It was generally agreed that if such a chuckleheaded idea brought dollars to the community it was worth a try. The kids who'd been teased about the size of their ears in the sixties were the men and women who, in the late eighties, launched an intensive campaign to transform Vulcan into a world-class Trekkie tourist destination.

The first order of business was ears. Thousands of rubber Spock ears, made in Hong Kong and designed to fit over the human variety, flooded the town. They caught on like wildfire. Soon townsfolk were sporting them on the street. They even took the ears with them when they travelled, claiming to all who would listen that they were Vulcans, from the planet in 40 Eridani, a triple star system sixteen light years from Earth. Those who saw or heard of the ears soon made the trip to Vulcan for a pair of their own. The ears came in packages labelled "Vulcan, Alberta. Just a speck on the map," with "speck" crossed out and "Spock" written in its place. Within two years more than 7,000 pairs sold. They remain a hot item today.

Town businesses flew with the new theme, prominently displaying life-sized cutouts of Spock, famously played by actor Leonard Nimoy, on their premises, and painting other characters from the series on their windows. Some businesses adopted new names, like Spock's Bar, the Enterprise Family Restaurant, and Starfleet Engineering. Murals depicting outer space and scenes from *Star Trek* appeared on public buildings. A liaison with Paramount Pictures was struck up to see about acquiring original props and sets, and soon it was known far and wide that the *Star Trek* theme town in southern Alberta was no joke.

Almost every town in the west hosts an annual fair or rodeo, a nod to pioneer days when settlers enjoyed the rare chance to socialize, and ranchers could show off their skills with roping and riding broncs and bulls. In short order, the name of Vulcan's rodeo was changed to Spock Days, paralleling Gene Roddenberry's space frontier with Canada's western frontier.

The uniqueness of the idea, the enthusiastic cooperation of town residents, and the sheer volume of *Trek* fans worldwide combined to bring curiosity-seekers to the community. Response was so good that in 1993 Vulcan hosted a *Star Trek* convention, VulCON I, attracting flocks of costumed Trekkies of all stripes and flooding the town with aliens for an entire weekend. To draw publicity for the event, Vulcan collaborated with another small Alberta town with spacey ideas. St. Paul had chosen to celebrate

Canada's 1967 centennial by building a UFO landing pad bearing a sign that reads, in part, "all visitors from earth or otherwise are welcome to this territory." Unfortunately, no extraterrestrial visitors had yet accepted the invitation. Two weeks prior to VulCON I, the media reported that a strange landing had occurred on the pad: a three-metre-long replica of the starship *USS Enterprise*. Some may have wondered if further landings might take place as word spread of an intergalactic convention on planet Earth. Indeed, Vulcan soon confirmed rumours that an invasion force of Klingons (a warrior species from the planet Qo'noS) was planning to transport down and sabotage the convention. Apparently they'd invaded once before and kidnapped the mayor, so Vulcans were on their guard. (It's unclear whether the invasion materialized, just as it's unclear whether offering a Klingon makeup workshop at the event was meant to appease or outwit the threatening species.)

The convention was a hit and became an annual affair. Two years later, Vulcan erected its own starship along the local highway—the *FX6–1995–A*—publicly proclaiming the theme of the town to all who passed. Its cairn-like pedestal bears greetings in three languages: English, Vulcan, and Klingon. There was no turning back. That same year, plans were approved to construct a space-age Tourism and Trek Station. More than a tourist booth, its unique shape is modeled after a futuristic spacecraft coming in for a landing, complete with coloured lights. Stepping inside the building, conversely, is like stepping outside the spacecraft and into outer space. Visitors find themselves transported into a starry cocoon populated with eerily lifelike, full-sized cutouts of the crew of the *Enterprise*. The building was completed in 1998, and while it functions as an accredited tourist centre with professionally trained staff and all the usual services visitor information centres provide (Vulcan is near two world-class heritage sites: Blackfoot Crossing and Head-Smashed-In Buffalo Jump), there is a heavy emphasis on science fiction and *Star Trek*. Staff dress in Starfleet uniforms and refer to themselves as captain and crew. Visitors can dress in similar costumes and pose for pictures with the immortalized-in-cardboard original cast. Dozens of Vulcan and *Star Trek* souvenirs are available for purchase (including uniforms and the ever-popular Vulcan ears). In addition, a collection of almost 1,000 items of memorabilia, donated by an avid fan, are on display. Particularly impressive are space age features such as a holodeck door which slides silently and majestically open, just like in the films, and a replica of the main bridge of the *Enterprise*.

As word spread of the small prairie community with the *Star Trek* connection, people from all over the world made inquiries and came to investigate, some in unusual ways. In 2004 a pair of Klingons chose Vulcan as the place in which to exchange Klingon wedding vows ("Today you are no longer alone"). They and forty of their closest friends attended the legal ceremony dressed in Klingon attire and later partook of a wedding feast of uniquely Klingon fare. The event received widespread media coverage, as did a similar *Star Trek*-themed wedding in 2010. On the other end of the spectrum, an out-of-town fan requested, and was granted, burial in the Vulcan, Alberta cemetery, under a gravestone shaped like the *Star Trek* insignia.

It might have been easy for the town to rest on their name and simply watch the tourists and their dollars roll in. The population jumped from 1,422 in 1990 to 1,940 in 2006, an impressive 27 per cent growth. But as Vulcan's reputation grew, the town kept pace. VulCON and Spock Days were amalgamated into a bigger event featuring more activities, and special guests from original movies and shows. VulCON 16: Spock Days/Galaxyfest 2009 featured no fewer than four notable *Trek* actors and a longtime script coordinator/producer's assistant from a total of five movies and fourteen series episodes. Remarkably, the event successfully merged science fiction with the down-home country feel of a small-town fair. The standard beef-on-a-bun barbecue, beer gardens, ball tournament, and interdenominational church service melded seamlessly with the 20th Anniversary KAG (Klingon Assault Group) national fan club Grand Assembly, costumed aliens, a *Star Trek* trade fair and art exhibit, special celebrity events (performance, autograph signings, Q&A sessions) and a masquerade party. Further examples of the ease with which a country fair and a space theme can combine appeared in the parade, the Shave-a-Klingon fundraiser for Kids Cancer Care, fireworks, family movie night (featuring the film *Trekkies*) and skydiving. Aliens and Trekkers alike enjoyed the pancake breakfast, bake sales, bed races, and family fun fair, mingling right alongside ordinary folk who didn't need to be familiar with *Star Trek*—or like it if they were—to find much to see, do, and appreciate.

Tourist numbers continued to climb, and in 2007 the Tourism and Trek Station, which was open year round, installed a new, state-of-the-art feature. The Vulcan Space Adventure Virtual Reality Game replicates in 3-D splendour the experience of being at the helm of the Starship *Enterprise*. Costumed players take over the controls and match wits with authentic characters approved for use by Paramount Pictures. The game clinched the station's identity as much more than a tourist booth.

In the same year, Vulcan launched a campaign to host the world movie premiere of J.J. Abrams' highly anticipated *Star Trek* reboot. For most tiny communities in rural Canada, the thought of attempting such a high-profile event would be unimaginable. But not for the people of Vulcan. They'd stepped beyond the bounds of believability many times already. They couldn't lose, they figured: if they didn't get the premiere, they'd get a whole lot of attention trying. And that's exactly what happened. Paramount Pictures took the serious proposal seriously. They even set up a conference call between Paramount executives and the Vulcan tourism coordinator. The town of Vulcan located the special equipment they'd need to run the film and had contractors ready to renovate the school gymnasium into a theatre. Ultimately Paramount killed the proposal, citing the lack of a proper movie theatre and enough lead time to put appropriate facilities in place. They did, however, promise to mention the town at the premiere and they invited Vulcan Tourism to attend a promotional screening prior to the movie's public release in May 2009. Despite initial disappointment, Vulcan was satisfied with .the campaign, which involved Facebook, YouTube, and media attention from around the world. China, Kuwait, Africa, Indonesia, Singapore, and France were just a few of the many countries to run stories about the quirky little town in southern Alberta.

Secure in the knowledge that their failed mission had in fact somewhat succeeded, Vulcans put the matter to rest. Then, on a Thursday morning in March 2009, Trek Station coordinator Dayna Dickens picked up the phone to discover Leonard Nimoy on the other end. Spock was phoning home. The station gets many prank calls, so Dayna was professionally polite while she waited for the punch line. But as the call progressed, there didn't seem to be one. Nimoy explained he'd been on the Internet and come across a story about Vulcan's campaign to premiere the new *Star Trek* movie in a town named for his character's home planet. He thought the idea was fantastic and urged the town of Vulcan to reignite its efforts. He then backed up his claim by contacting major media outlets and calling Paramount. The following day the phones were busy as Dayna Dickens received confirmation that the real Leonard Nimoy had indeed initiated the calls. Efforts to bring the premiere to Vulcan were renewed with fresh verve and some serious clout. The town with the crazy theme and zany ideas hit the press once more.

Paramount took note. Logistically, they still didn't feel they could bring the premiere to Vulcan, but they could do the next best thing: they would provide transportation and foot the tab for 300 Vulcan and county residents to attend a private advance screening of the new Star Trek film at a Calgary theatre, two days before its worldwide release. In addition, Bruce Greenwood, the actor playing the role of Captain Christopher Pike in the film, would make a guest appearance. Vulcan ran a free lottery to select the lucky 300, and on May 6, 2009, three posh buses arrived to transport Vulcans, many of them elaborately costumed, to the viewing. Stepping off at their Calgary destination was like stepping onto a Hollywood red carpet as media from numerous networks, armed with microphones and cameras, assailed the intergalactic travellers. Flashbulbs flared as the visitors from Vulcan made their way to the screening room. It was a stellar moment in the quest of little Vulcan, Alberta, to keep its name on the map.

That summer, tourism numbers spiked to the highest they'd ever been. Shortly afterwards, Vulcan was dubbed the *Star Trek* Capital of Canada and, after months of negotiation, was licensed by the television network CBS as an official *Star Trek* destination. This freed them to sell *Star Trek*-branded products without fear of lawsuits for copyright infringement. Soon they will launch a line of licensed collectibles, and plans are underway to create and market their own *Star Trek* products (Vulcan jerky and *Star Trek* bottled water among them).

Since the day he discovered a facsimile of his home planet on Earth, Leonard Nimoy has been lending his name and support to Vulcan's ongoing endeavours. Little did he know that Spock's childhood pet, the bear-cat Sehlat, had been in Vulcan all along, acting as mascot for the town and quite possibly waiting for its master to come home. The two finally reunited in April 2010, when Spock (in the guise of Nimoy) "returned home" to Vulcan, courtesy of the Calgary Comic and Entertainment Expo.

To say Vulcan, Alberta is on a roll in terms of publicity and notoriety would be an understatement. But those who do not live there will be surprised to learn that the community is anything but fantastical. Agriculture is still Vulcan's economic mainstay, and for most of the year it functions as a typical farming community. When no aliens, tourists, or television cameras lurk, residents put away their ears, and thoughts of *Star Trek* are light years away. A summer student working the tourist booth confesses that though she grew up in Vulcan she's never watched a single episode of *Star Trek*, and nobody she knows has any interest in the show. When emails started arriving at the station in Klingon, the staff had to scramble to find a Klingon dictionary. Even then, it took ages to decipher the code.

Even though the town logo now features a spacecraft swooping around a single grain elevator on the edge of a prairie town, and even though letters are cancelled at the Vulcan post office with a stamp in the shape of a space station, a peek at the town website reveals that it downplays the *Star Trek* connection when it comes to attracting business and new residents, focusing instead on the agricultural fertility of the area and the benefits of small town living.

The occasional opportunity for space-related promotion aside, Vulcan really only explodes into full-blown alien mode one weekend a year. It's a farming community blessed with a name and a sense of humour perfectly blended for a little fun on the side. In Vulcan's case, however, the "little fun on the side" has morphed into worldwide recognition, hundreds of thousands of tourists, and millions of dollars.

When they meet or depart, those on the dry, dusty, fictional planet of Vulcan—a peaceful society of farmers—exchange the blessing, "Live long and prosper." For their counterparts on Earth, also existing in a dry, dusty, agricultural environment, the blessing has been fulfilled.

Chapter 9
Lynn Lake

Lynn Lake

Giving Up The Ghost

In 2004, a reader sent Emil Szekrenyes, author of the newsletter "Lynn Lake, A Town to Remember," a fistful of pages from the telephone directory, along with the comment, "As you can see, Lynn Lake is still in the phone book. It is not just 'a place to remember'.... There are feasts at the Friendship Centre to celebrate Thanksgiving and Christmas. The Legion fills for dinners and dances. July 1st has a parade and bbq downtown."

Emil's response was sympathetic but firm. "We all know," he wrote, "that [Lynn Lake is] coping with the hard reality of being a single industry community whose zenith passed three decades ago. I need not elaborate on the struggle. None of us... wish to refer to the community in the past tense. The people living there, choosing to remain there, are a hardy lot, continuing in the spirit that put Lynn Lake on the map in the late 1940s. [It is] a viable community that is trying to sustain itself through whatever resourceful endeavors it can muster."

Sherritt Gordon Mines Ltd. fathered the Town of Lynn Lake, 1,100 kilometres north of Winnipeg, Manitoba, in the early 1950s and for almost thirty years nurtured it like a cherished child. Every need of its residents was met, which was no small feat in the northern wilderness with no road or rail service, no television or radio, and only a few public phone booths with which to communicate with the outside world—or rather, to place an order with the commissary at the mine for the next bush plane coming in with supplies. In an effort to establish a permanent, settled community, Sherritt Gordon offered unprecedented incentives to attract young couples with families: training, higher than average wages, and generous financing to buy or build homes. It worked. Far from being a typical, makeshift mining camp of tents and portable huts, Lynn Lake was a properly planned town with churches, a hospital, school, post office, bank, stores, and recreational facilities. Thanks to the company's vision, Lynn Lake evolved as a tightly knit community with a family atmosphere. And Sherritt Gordon enjoyed a stable, loyal workforce.

It's remarkable that this happy, thriving community was carved from the trees, rocks, and bush of the remote north, where winter freeze-ups and spring thaws isolate people from the world for weeks at a time. It's even more remarkable that the town had been lifted—physically—from Sherritt

Gordon's first mining location, Sherridon.

When copper ore began to deplete in the Sherridon mine just a few years after it opened, the company stepped up exploration efforts for new deposits. In 1941, many kilometres north, a company geologist identified nickel on an outcropping of rock surrounded by muskeg, swamp, and bush near a little lake named Lynn, after Sherritt Gordon's chief engineer. The find was significant, but Canada was then embroiled in the Second World War, and much of the material and manpower needed to open a new mine was unavailable.

Company officials knew that making the discovery public would trigger a rush of prospectors to the area. They needed to keep the nickel's existence confidential until they had the resources to detect its richest deposits and secure claims on them. It is a testament to the loyalty Sherritt Gordon inspired in its employees that the secret was never leaked. Instead, as the war progressed, they quietly went about laying the groundwork to develop what turned out to be one of the largest nickel strikes on the continent.

When the war ended in 1945, the company wasted no time staking the first of 344 claims in a thirty-square-mile area. It was poised to move its operation from Sherridon to Lynn Lake.

How to get it there was the first great challenge. The terrain was clotted with muskeg, trees, and brush and barriered by lakes, ravines, and rocky ridges. It was not difficult to fly men in, but transporting heavy machinery and building material by air was out of the question. So was building a conventional road. Instead, the company was forced to hack a trail through the bush to create a winter road.

The road was passable only after temperatures dropped low enough to freeze the lakes and muskeg and sufficient snow had fallen to cover stumps and rocks. To navigate the 193 kilometres between Sherridon and Lynn Lake, tractor trains laden with supplies had to creep laboriously over 265 kilometres of packed ice.

By 1947, about twenty advance families living in tents and one-room huts were on site sinking shafts and setting up buildings and equipment. As copper ore dwindled in the Sherridon mine and operations wound down, men were transferred to Lynn Lake where they lived in bunkhouses (termed "ram pastures") until their families could join them.

The company's next great challenge was rendering an environment in which families could live comfortably. Surveyors were hired to map out a town, and plans got underway to build it. However, Sherritt Gordon soon discovered the exorbitant costs of purchasing and hauling in materials for construction. Realizing that the superstructure they needed for a new town already existed in the old one being left behind, the company made a decision. As company president Eldon Brown announced, "Sherridon won't become a ghost town. We'll take the ghost with us."

Those who are superstitious might not think it's a good idea to take a ghost with you. Nevertheless, thus began an epic undertaking the likes of which, as far as anyone knew, had never been attempted before.

Beginning in 1948, it took the Patricia Transportation Company Ltd. six consecutive winters to carry the buildings of Sherridon to their new home in Lynn Lake. The operation could only take place in deepest cold, when the ice was at least two feet thick and capable of supporting the twenty-two-ton swings, each consisting of three heavy tractors pulling up to eighteen sleds loaded with equipment and supplies. A single sled bringing up the rear carried one building. The swings travelled continuously. Their crew of six drivers and two brakemen split into shifts to keep the convoy moving, averaging a snail's pace of less than six kilometres an hour. Stopping for any reason in the extreme cold—even to refuel—was courting disaster. Each swing had a wooden caboose in which the men slept between shifts. A cook manning a wood-burning stove kept them fed. The caboose was the only shelter they had for the entire 265-kilometre, three-day journey. Once the swing arrived in Lynn Lake it dropped its load, hooked onto the empty sleds from the previous trip, and began heading back within the hour.

The trip was treacherous, with tons of dynamite on board; temperatures dipped as low as minus-fifty degrees, and steep ravines threatened disastrous runaways. It's a marvel that throughout the relocation only one tractor fell through the ice (killing the driver); only one building, the massive United Church, came close to sinking (a startled tractor driver saw the tidal wave looming behind him and gave full throttle to pull the church to safety) and only one caboose caught fire (leaving the off shift stranded in their underwear until help miraculously arrived). Other than that, the 182 homes hauled across the rough and frozen terrain suffered nary a crack nor a toppled chimney.

While the community was being moved, up to eight swings were in use at one time, but once the town was settled, only one swing came each winter, bringing food, clothing, lumber, machinery, and equipment. It was impossible to travel overland the rest of the year, when swamps and muskeg would have swallowed anything attempting to traverse them. Until an airport was built, mail and perishable food were flown in once a week by bush plane, but only if lakes were frozen or open enough to land a ski or float plane. Every family had to order a year's worth of supplies in advance, and for a portion of the year houses were crammed with groceries—stuffed under beds, behind furniture, into closets, and up the walls.

Life in Lynn Lake was good. By all accounts, children growing up there were happy. The isolation, extreme weather, absence of radio and television—even the dastardly summer mosquitoes and blackflies—threw everyone together. "One of the first buildings erected by volunteer labour was the curling rink," states Lynn Lake resident Elaine Baribeau in her essay *A Town on Skids*. "Of the 200 people in the community, 196 belonged to the curling club."

Over the years, the atypical living conditions spawned some extraordinary individuals, including National Hockey League and 2010 Olympics coach Mike Babcock and award-winning singer/songwriter Tom Cochrane. With the creation of *For Better or For Worse*, the well-known comic strip series, illustrator Lynn Johnston came into her own in Lynn Lake in the late 1970s. She credits her time there for the popular First Nations storyline she eventually produced, which earned her high praise and induction into the Order of Manitoba.

In 1949, Sherritt Gordon Mines and Canadian National Railways negotiated an extension of The Pas/Sherridon branch line to Lynn Lake. As grateful as passengers were for the service, the trip on the new rail line was anything but smooth. "The train ride on the 'Muskeg Special' was 12 hours of stops, lurches, sways," writes Baribeau, "all over muskeg and around bends… rocks, lakes scrawny trees and rugged terrain…. The train crawled along, so slow at times one could have walked as fast." Though it was hardly punctual, the train was soon chugging into town three times a week.

It took another dozen years for communication barriers to further open with the arrival of radio broadcasts and "canned" television in 1966 and 1967. With great excitement, households scrambled to acquire radios and television sets. Often neighbours gathered together to watch the four hours per day of television programming taped in black and white and aired a week after the original broadcast. Live TV didn't arrive until five years later, at which point Saturday evening community events were suspended so people could stay home and watch *Hockey Night in Canada*.

Lynn Lake grew steadily larger and busier. The coming of the railroad opened opportunities for commercial fishing and made Lynn Lake the major market centre for the region.

Air traffic in and out was accomplished by bush plane and company charter, but the service was erratic and expensive. By 1970 Lynn Lake had a full-service airport, and aviator Carl Arnold Lawrence Morberg brought to the community the company he named after his own initials. Soon Calm Air had fourteen planes running regularly scheduled freight and passenger service to and from the community. Town residents now enjoyed reliable, ready access to almost anything they desired, including a daily newspaper from Winnipeg.

As Sherritt Gordon Mines Ltd. continued exploration and expansion, the town boomed. Housing was so scarce that newcomers were grateful to find lodging in someone's garage. With the opening of the Fox Lake copper/zinc mine in 1970, Sherritt Gordon began hiring women for all positions. In many households both partners were on the company payroll. New houses, late-model cars, trailers, and boats peppered the streets and lanes. "Where ptarmigan and spruce grouse once fed, apartment buildings erupted," writes Baribeau. "A new housing development ploughed under the best blueberry patch."

The discovery of copper at nearby Ruttan Lake portended yet another mine, as did Sherritt Gordon's venture into gold mining. The future was airtight bright. Or so it seemed.

The town of Lynn Lake was so prosperous and was advancing so rapidly that some worried its original pioneering spirit, born of the hardships of the early years, would fade into distant memory and disappear. Lynn Lake locals seemed to have forgotten a spirit of another kind that hovered. Almost 200 kilometres south, all that remained were crumbling foundations, a few forlorn shacks, and an old, bewildered-looking hotel. "We'll take the ghost with us," Sherritt Gordon's president had said. Those with foresight might have sensed something ominous in those words. The legacy of Sherridon, a dismantled, deserted mining town, hung like a pall over its creation.

"There's never been any doubts in people's minds that this was a town with a future," local businessman Walter Perepeluk said in an interview with the *Winnipeg Tribune* in 1970. "One of the main reasons for the area's success is Sherritt Gordon... The company and the town pull in the same direction. What's good for the town is good for the company, and there never has been any problems here."

But the mining industry has always had its ups and downs. Ore quality, extraction difficulties, market fluctuations, and mined-out operations are all hurdles, as is the challenge of attracting families willing to settle in remote locations. Mining companies in general began flying workers from urban areas into mining camps for fourteen-day shifts. Sherritt Gordon followed suit, hiring temporary crews that flew in and out and didn't set down roots. By the mid-1970s the originally developed mine sites had tapped out. In 1985, the Fox Mine reached the end of its lifespan. That same year, Calm Air pulled up stakes and moved its headquarters to Thompson, a larger northern community. Two years later, in 1987, Sherritt Gordon sold out to LynnGold Resources Inc., effectively severing ties with the town it had created. Perepeluk's confident assertion disintegrated. The company and the town no longer pulled together.

Lynn Lakers were jarred but still optimistic. There was plenty of nickel, copper, zinc, and gold left to mine. It just needed overseeing. The parent they had relied upon with such trust, however, was gone, and within two years LynnGold declared bankruptcy, leaving a large percentage of the population out of work. The town was devastated.

Over the ensuing years other mining companies came, plundered the earth, and left. Eventually mining ceased completely. From a high of 3,500 people in 1975, Lynn Lake's population steadily declined. By 2001, it had dropped to 699. The town was dying and—severely compromised by contamination from the mines—so was everything around it.

Lynn Lake was faced with a double catastrophe: the town's very soul and purpose had been stripped away, and toxins left from abandoned mines were poisoning the environment. If the community was going to survive, it needed to both rehabilitate the land and redefine its identity.

Residents had always enjoyed the bounty and beauty of their surroundings. There were numerous nearby lakes, around which they built cottages; they hiked, snowmobiled, hunted, and fished. The magnificence of the boreal forests and the majesty of the northern lights were theirs, to the extent that they even resented the intrusion when outsiders appeared to fish the lakes and pursue the plentiful game.

Jim MacLellan, objecting to the opening of a highway between Lynn Lake and Thompson in 1970, told the *Winnipeg Tribune*, "When I first moved here with my wife, we could drive a short way out of town and catch a few fish and enjoy ourselves. As soon as the tourist comes, the lakes are fished more and it becomes tougher to find good fishing holes. I'm not against progress, but there are priorities for individuals and some people feel that you can overdevelop an area."

This approach was fine as long as the mines were productive and the economy strong. But when they closed the need to rethink and refocus was clear. Tourists had been trickling in for years. Already there were several fly-in lodges in the area. As a regional service centre with all the amenities already in place—food, fuel, hardware, hospital, airport and access to anything else one might need—the people of Lynn Lake knew they were uniquely positioned to promote a special kind of tourism.

Residents undertook an inventory of the gifts their region offered. A wide variety of plant species, eskers left over from the ice age, and stands of stunted spruce (which had already earned the area the nickname "Land of Little Sticks") were curiosities that opened up possibilities for eco-tourism. Hiking, camping, boating, and all manner of snow sports (including dogsledding) were popular activities that could be expanded upon. As a natural habitat for grey owls, eagles, timber wolves, caribou, moose, fox, black and coloured bear, and many other kinds of wildlife, the area was attractive to nature lovers of all stripes.

With the presence of outfitters and fly-in lodges, hunting and fishing had been simmering on the back burner of Lynn Lake's economy for some time. But as long as there was mining, locals hadn't cared to stir the tourism pot. Now they brought it forward and turned up the heat. "Lynn Lake: mining company town," became "Lynn Lake: Portal to Adventure," offering outdoor activities for every taste, from bear hunting to birdwatching—and especially fishing. Trophy-sized lake trout, walleye, and northern pike in at least eleven world-class fishing lakes within minutes of the town amply justified the new designation: "Sportfishing Capital of Manitoba." A new logo was designed, featuring a mine in the background, flanked by forest and lake, with a large fish leaping skyward in the foreground.

Today, Lynn Lake still honours its heritage with the Lynn Lake Mining Town Museum, and mining companies continue to explore one of the most promising mineral belts in Canada. However, the town promotes itself almost exclusively as a tourist destination highlighting the unique ruggedness and beauty of the true north. Roughly two dozen fishing lodges and no fewer than five outfitters operate in the area. The focus on a northern aesthetic includes the many First Nations and Métis people in the region, whose cultures are celebrated and showcased through special events and more than a dozen murals in the community.

The one blot overshadowing Lynn Lake's success has been the contaminated earth. The mine sites may have vanished, but the toxins in the soil remain, killing vegetation and preventing new growth. When wet, they liquefy into a vile sludge not unlike battery acid and turn water a noxious, alien red. When dry they are a fine dust, easily airborne. They corrode everything they come into contact with.

"It's like the day after a nuclear holocaust," Mayor Audie Dulewich told the *Winnipeg Free Press* in September 2006. "It makes it very difficult to promote the town for other things, like tourism."

Current government regulations ensure that mining companies build site remediation into their business plans, but when Sherritt Gordon and its successors operated in the Lynn Lake area, the need for environmental stewardship was not recognized. When mines became no longer viable, companies simply walked away, leaving the tailings from abandoned or orphaned sites to do their damage. Ultimately Lynn Lake was deemed one of the five most contaminated areas in the province. Pilots flying tourists over otherwise stunning scenery tended to avoid the spots where the view of lifeless landscapes and red lakes was disturbing and surreal. Constant lobbying of government and mining company officials for rehabilitation took years to produce results. A 2001 Human and Environmental Health Risk Assessment initiated by the Manitoba government and undertaken over a portion of the contaminated area concluded that "the exposures to metals in the environment are not expected to result in adverse human health effects for people living in the town over a lifetime." Nevertheless, residents noted an unusually high incidence of Crohn's disease and disturbing cancer clusters. In one dramatic case, nineteen people within a two-block radius, some only in their twenties or thirties, developed cancer.

Naturally, town growth was impeded. Due to the sick land, the Marcel Colomb First Nation chose not to establish a new urban reserve in the community.

Finally, in 2006, the Manitoba government announced a $70 million program to rehabilitate contaminated mine sites, and work got underway to heal the land. Remediation and reclamation will take a minimum of ten years. On the bright side, it requires people, which means employment and increased economic activity bringing money back into the community while new, more eco-friendly mine development takes place.

In 2010, at approximately 800 people (and more during the summer months) the population of Lynn Lake is on the rise again.

Ironically, the name of the first child born in the community told the story of the town's fortunes. His first name, "Lynn," honoured the bright new community, full of promise; but his last name, "Hunt," forecast the surprising change of direction that would ultimately save the town.

The ghost of Sherridon can never be exorcised from Lynn Lake, but with land rehabilitation underway, tourism firmly established, mineral exploration ongoing, and advanced mining techniques developed, the spectre need no longer be feared.

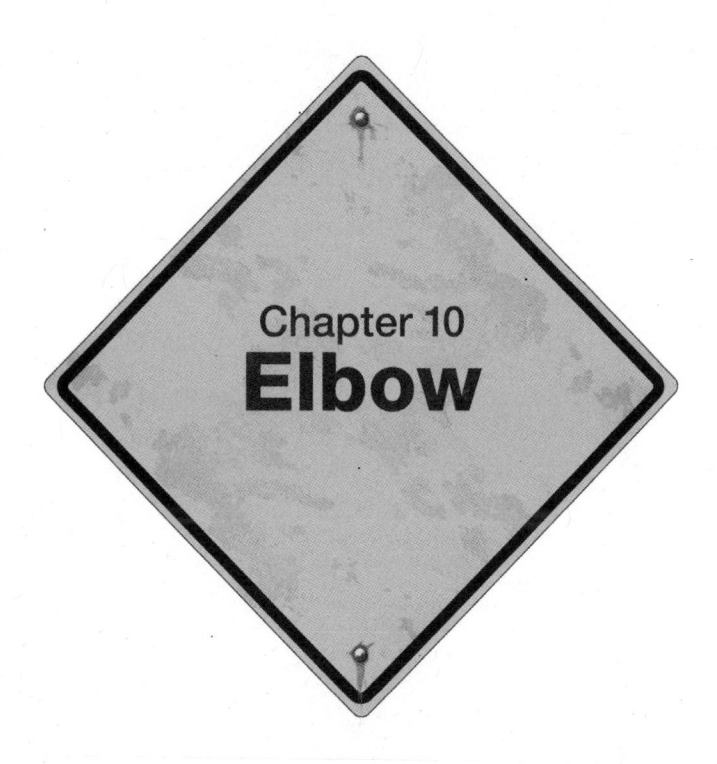

Chapter 10
Elbow

Elbow

Sailing In or Elbowed Out?

In the spring of 2002 Marjorie McPhee and her husband, Wayne Berry, were looking for a place to try out a boat they were hauling from Ontario back home to Calgary, Alberta.

"We thought, 'Why don't we see if there's any water at all in Saskatchewan?'" says Marjorie. "We didn't know Saskatchewan from a hole in the ground." As she studied the map, an interesting blue configuration caught her eye, and while Wayne gassed up in Chaplin, Marjorie told the station attendant, "We stopped in Moosomin and asked, and I phoned Regina Tourism, and nobody seems to know [about] this 'J' shape in the middle of the province."

The attendant breathed a reverent sigh as he recognized Diefenbaker Lake. "Oh *yeeeeaaah*. You've got to go to

Riverhurst!" he said, and promptly gave directions.

When Wayne and Marjorie arrived at the Riverhurst marina they were stunned to discover a body of water 225 kilometres long and almost 60 feet deep, skirted by 800 kilometres of sandy shoreline. They spent five glorious days on the lake. Resuming their journey after the unscheduled interlude, they marvelled at their good fortune.

"We realized we'd probably come through that area three or four times and missed Lake Diefenbaker altogether."

The couple owns a business buying and refurbishing boats for resale. Thanks to their Ontario broker, they soon found themselves on another trip. "We picked up a trawler near Kenora to take down south to Florida, and Wayne said, 'Why don't we go back to Riverhurst and put her in there?'"

"I'm really looking at this map and it says there's another marina," replied Marjorie. "Let's be daring and go to Elbow."

It was daring indeed, for the route took them over a narrow, gravelly highway heaving with cracks and potholes. Marjorie chuckles as she recalls their gamble. "Brand new truck, brand new boat. Oh dear God!"

The road to Elbow was not always so neglected. The town used to be on a main thoroughfare. Today the map locates it on the crossbar of a J-shaped lake, but before 1959 it was at the elbow of an arm-shaped river—hence its name. Elbow was incorporated in 1909 and thrived for twenty years before falling hard during the Great Depression. It was still a regional market centre, but like many small communities dependent upon agriculture, it had difficulty recovering. Even during the relative prosperity of the Second

World War and the years following it, the town struggled. Naturally, then, most residents were pleased when plans were announced in 1958 to bring irrigation to the region, even though it meant damming the South Saskatchewan River and flooding the valley. Optimism ran high, but the cost was dear. It wasn't just prized gooseberry patches and favourite picnic spots that disappeared underwater. An ancient site sacred to the indigenous peoples, a Bible camp, and entire farms were lost.

"It was so beautiful down there," says Sue Cafferata, who owns the Lakeview Lodge Motel with her husband, Keith Daniluk. "Now it's all underwater."

Joan Soggie agrees. She moved to Elbow from nearby Beechy three years before the flood. "As a university student I took the bus home from Saskatoon and we'd cross the river at Elbow. I'd be glued to the window, it was so pretty. There was a curvy road, and steep river banks covered with trees. In the fall it was spectacular with all the colours in the late afternoon sunshine. I felt sad to think it was all going to be flooded. There were people who had beautiful homes overlooking the river, built fifty years before. The hills were bulldozed, the trees pushed out. It was all done in the name of progress."

Among the casualties was the bridge, the main artery carrying people and commerce in and out of the community. As the flooding turned the river into a lake this vital life flow was diverted to the town of Outlook. Outlook grew strong, and Elbow atrophied.

But not before a last hurrah. Construction of the South

Saskatchewan Dam northwest of the community began in 1959. The project required so much manpower that the town of Cutbank was created to house workers. They overflowed into Elbow, and to everyone's delight the town boomed for eight years. That's when Sue's parents moved from Moose Jaw and opened a motel.

"Motels and cabins were built just to accommodate the workers," says Joan. "There was work for everybody."

In 1966, the dam was renamed the Gardiner Dam, in honour of former Saskatchewan premier James G. Gardiner. It was dedicated in 1967— and just like that, the boom was over. The Cafferatas left the motel business and Sue's father went to work helping develop Douglas Provincial Park. The stage was set for a new era of agricultural prosperity; however, the expected benefits of the dam didn't materialize.

"When there weren't irrigation ditches proposed for this area it meant that the irrigation wasn't going to be a big thing here," states Joan. "It was only applicable to those who could access the water. A lot of people who started found it was not for them because of the high cost of power. And some of the land is so sandy it can take any amount of water and any amount of fertilizer. Most people continued dryland farming.

"But there was the deep-water coulee that would be good for a marina."

The magnificent Diefenbaker Lake was not an average reservoir, and residents were quick to recognize and build upon its recreational potential. The psychological shift from farming community to resort village was relatively easy, especially as the new provincial park began drawing tourists.

"I remember the older folks commenting in a kind of pleased way that they'd go into the store and hardly recognize anyone because there were so many strangers in town," says Joan. "They didn't want the town to change overnight—nobody wants their hometown to change so they don't recognize it—but it was always nice to see that other people found the town attractive, or found some reason to come here."

The lake quickly gained a reputation as a great place to swim, boat, fish, water-ski, and generally frolic in the sun and sand. Sailing and windsurfing were particularly appealing. The lake's size and unique shape afforded opportunities to catch the wind in three different directions, virtually guaranteeing a good sail on any given day. Elbow embraced the fun-seekers warmly. An RV park, campsites, and picnic areas were developed, and a top-notch eighteen-hole golf course built. Things really took off when hometown boys Bryan and Barry Cafferata opened a marina in 1986. Today the 150-slip marina is always full.

As a safety precaution, and to protect the environment, development is prohibited along the shoreline. As a result, vacation amenities are concentrated within the village. Rental cabins and condominiums have been built, bed and breakfast establishments flourish, and quirky little shops catering to resort tourism dot Main Street. Travellers approaching on the highway from either direction encounter unique, sailboat-shaped signs advertising village services and urging visitors to "sail into Elbow."

And they do just that, undeterred by the ongoing challenge of the road. Built decades ago, it was never intended for modern tractor trailer units, farm trucks, and other heavy machinery common on today's highways. Even with continual patching and repair, it deteriorates each spring. However, the problem has been well-aired and efforts to address it are underway, possibly hastened by the agitation of some members of the RCMP when their cruiser lost a wheel and axle to a pothole.

One would think that such road conditions would deter people from coming to Elbow, but it isn't just the lake that keeps drawing them back; an atmosphere of friendly welcome permeates the town. Elbow's website asserts that the community is "a quiet prairie village, where neighbours value each other and extend friendly greetings to strangers, rightly assuming that they are likely 'just neighbours they have not met yet.'"

This statement is not an exaggeration. I arrived at midnight on a summer's eve. Sue, from the motel, waited up for me after I called to say I was running late. She left her home in the middle of the night to come down and register me in a room. Despite the inconvenience (she had four children and another job to get to in the morning), she took the time to chat under the glow of a streetlamp. The next day I strolled grass-cracked sidewalks down gravelled streets and couldn't help but absorb the community's cozy, small-town hominess. Many of the houses were older, set in well-landscaped yards bursting with bloom. Hovering like bees among the foliage were people engaged in the day-today activities of their lives. Every one of them acknowledged me. Down one street a woman stretched up from clipping a spray of flowers and sang out a greeting.

"Hello! Nice day, isn't it? I hope the laundry dries on the line before any rain hits." She was as familiar with me as if we'd been neighbours for years.

At the next house an elderly lady in a flowered dress and straw hat sat in repose on her veranda, almost hidden among banks of potted flowers. In her cheery "Hello!" I heard the shy but unmistakable invitation, "Come and sit awhile." Trees were in full leaf; sweet peas laced thickly through trellises; the air was alive with birdsong. On the next street a young mother with a watering can bent over planters snugged up against her small house. The white frame building, lovingly trimmed with purple, stood almost flush with the sidewalk, where a matching purple bench waited to give rest.

"Hi there," she said.

Nobody in Elbow knew who I was, yet everybody was willing to talk. I realized I was experiencing what the website claims.

Residents are aware of their roles as hosts and are always on the lookout for ways to better meet the needs of their guests. Local people initiated many of the tourist-based businesses. Some changed almost exclusively from agriculture to tourism for their livelihoods. Others branched out to run businesses on the side. For a time, Joan and her husband ran a B&B. She regrets that they eventually had to give it up.

"I just loved it," she says. "But we were farming a lot of land at the time and I was also working at the school. It was very busy."

While residents had no problem promoting the town's recreational attributes, even switching hats to cater to the tourists, it was less easy to watch others move in to take advantage of Elbow's charms for their own economic benefit. "Most of the businesses that have just started are people that have come here because they want to retire," says Joan. "It's a good place to retire. They feel they can have a little business to make life interesting. I think it's wonderful." But she admits that in close-knit rural communities, people generally need to prove themselves before they are trusted. "In a small town you stay a newcomer for a long time." She laughs as she relates her own experience. "I still feel like an outsider myself, lots of times… forty-two years later."

Marjorie and Wayne know that feeling of being an outsider. They too were retired when they started their boat refurbishing business in Calgary. On their very first trip to Elbow, the lake lovers recognized a phenomenon they'd seen before. "From the moment we came into this little town, the two of us were saying it was just like Sylvan Lake in 1975 when it hit that critical mass. People are looking for this; they're looking for water." At the time, due to a dry year, their own boat was "sitting on bottom" at the popular Alberta resort. On the lake at Elbow they "sailed all over the place and had an absolute blast." As they pulled out of town several days later, Wayne suddenly stopped the truck.

"That building's for sale," he said, gesturing to an empty

store on Main Street. "I wonder what the cost of real estate is like around here." The seed of an idea was germinating. "We got out and a lady came to talk to us from a garage sale she was having," says Marjorie. "We asked her how much she thought the building was and she suggested around $30,000. We thought she was talking in terms she didn't understand; it was probably $300,000. Two hours later we owned the store. We paid $28,000."

Marjorie and Wayne relocated their boat refurbishing business to Elbow. The Chinook Winds Boatique took wing, and soon expanded to sell lake apparel, boat accessories, marine equipment, and "anything nautical."

From the beginning the strangers were observed with curiosity and skepticism. "When we opened the store we went through an awful lot of hoops," Marjorie recalls. "In a small community, when people like Wayne and I come in and open up a store 'like that'"—she snaps her fingers—"they look at you and say, 'I don't like you, first off.'" She attributes this aversion to the general hardship suffered by farming communities everywhere. "Watching crops freeze... drown... come too early... infestation... equipment prices going so high you can't get your money back. [We were] doing something they can't attain...because [farming] always falls apart."

Fortunately Wayne and Marjorie met Henry Harms, a local man with an unshakeable belief in Elbow's future. He had taken others under his wing when they came to set up businesses. Now he welcomed the Berry-McPhees. Henry became a trusted friend. "He's been a guide; a great counsellor to us. He would say, 'Now this is what you need to think about when you're talking to so-and-so. And don't press that kind of button because it will drive them back.'"

Wayne, a former buildings manager for the University of Calgary, and Marjorie, a healthcare professional, were sensitive to the small town's subtle undercurrents and took their challenge to overcome local opposition in stride. Within a few months of opening the Boatique, they began thinking about a second business. An abandoned gas station caught Wayne's practiced eye. "I've walked all through it," he told Marjorie when he took her to see it. "It has the ability to stand and stay standing and be healthy. I think I'd like to develop it into something."

The old gas station was "up to its heinie in back taxes," says Marjorie. "It was a mess; it was an absolute disaster."

"What's holding you back?" she responded. "We did a one-dollar deal with the owner. The guy didn't even want the building. Then we ended up talking to Town Council, which was a bit of a struggle."

Were they moving too quickly? As outsiders, they hadn't yet gained the trust and rapport necessary to do business in a small town. Ultimately Council requested that the building be turned over to the town for back taxes, which Wayne and Marjorie would have to pay off in order to claim ownership. In exchange, they offered to clean up the property.

"Which is cool; that was a plus," says Marjorie. It took several months to get the taxes paid off, and in the meantime renovations began. Marjorie, who grew up in a small town, had a unique way of dealing with the inevitable naysayers.

When people wanted to know what they were doing with the rundown, overgrown site she glibly told them, "It's going to be a brothel and it's going to be called the Pink Palace."

"A community loves to have something to gossip about—to get their feathers all torn up over," she says. "If you stretch the imagination way out there, when you bring it back to reality it's easier to accept."

The reality was an upper-end restaurant with a menu that reflected the region. "We would like people to realize that Elbow is a recreation destination," Marjorie says. "The idea was to create a Muskoka-style boathouse restaurant. Keep the marine theme.

"You move people step by step by step," she continues. "The next step was to open the doors so the community could come in and see the progression." During renovations, curiosity-seekers often stopped by. If the timing was right, they got coffee and a seat swept of plaster and sawdust to sit and visit amid the construction chaos. Some members of the community even rolled up their sleeves and worked side by side with Wayne to get the building in shape. Gradually, and to Wayne and Marjorie's great delight, a sense of community ownership evolved. Today the Chinook Winds Boathouse Restaurant is in full swing, keeping pace with a town that is thriving.

Elbow's survival is significant, not just because it overcame the small-town temptation to close ranks against newcomers. It has also grappled with centralization, the harbinger of death for many small communities.

"We lost our post office about the same time we lost our

school," says Joan. "It almost seemed as though anything that was controlled outside the town was going to be taken away if it possibly could be." The rail line, too, is gone, and the elevator is closed. Even the valley was taken from them, but what they got in return was a lake, and what they did in response was something they could control.

The people of Elbow are well aware that keeping tourists happy is what keeps the town alive. In 2005, Muriel Peterson, owner of Second to None, a quality secondhand furniture and collectibles shop, told a *Star Phoenix* reporter, "Because we have a lot of summer visitors we can keep a grocery store, we can keep a bank, we can have several restaurants and we have new housing going up." Each spring the resident population nearly triples from the sedate 300 it's been for decades to over 800. Thousands more pour in for day trips, golfing, and beach vacations. Marjorie, Wayne, and others have proven their sincerity and loyalty to the little town and paved the way for others to do the same. In 2006, more than sixty lots were sold in the village. Between 2005 and 2010, numerous businesses opened, many by people discovering Elbow for the first time. In their descriptions of the people of the community, certain phrases appear again and again: "open minded," "people who have vision," "the spirit is great." Secure that the integrity of their lovely village will not be abused or compromised, the town now actively recruits new business. As their YouTube video testifies, "Elbow is open for business and ready for more entrepreneurs."

The wind is back in her sails.

Chapter 11
Warner

Warner

The Warriors of Warner

"What came first, the chicken or the egg?" The answer seems irrelevant to the people of Warner, Alberta. The rise of interpretive centres in other prairie communities needed the discovery of dinosaur skeletons, but Warner needed only prehistoric eggshells to prompt development of its museum, which celebrates the hadrosaur nesting site discovered nearby, as well as the community's heritage.

During the first half of the twentieth century, when one-room country schools fought against the centralization that would eventually make them extinct, Warner saw opportunity. Rather than lose its students to larger schools farther away, it built its own large school and became the hub of the first consolidated district in the province. When the Quonset erected to store a surplus of grain in the 1950s was no longer needed, Warner recycled it into a civic centre to which it added artificial ice in 1970. In 2001, when dwindling enrolment threatened the coveted school, Warner hatched a plan to save it by attracting young hockey players from around the world to live in the village, attend school, and play hockey in the decades-old Quonset-turned-civic centre. How they would pitch a hockey school to prospective student athletes without a program or a coach, and how they could attract a coach without a program or athletes were dismissed as chicken-and-egg issues. Irrelevant. Warner saw only opportunity and it acted.

This strength is remarkable for a village that is in every other sense unremarkable. Warner's 383 residents sit isolated at the bottom of the province, sixty-five kilometres southeast of Lethbridge. Few cars travel the rutted streets, most of which remain unpaved. Where pavement exists, it is pebbled and worn. Empty storefronts pock the wide main street. A forsaken church has cracked and broken windows. Old, storied, once-grand houses languish on large, loosely-kept lots. Smaller houses, just as thirsty for paint, tuck in amongst scraggly bushes. Bright, newer homes are less conspicuous. This is not a pretty town. It speaks of practical living and hard work. Its few frills are limited to Main Street, where hanging baskets of flowers soften the view during the summer months.

Near the west end of the village squats the school, a one-storey, brick-clad structure flanked by a well-equipped playground. A large field links the school with the civic centre/hockey rink on the west edge of town. The centre is typical of those in many prairie communities: a Quonset appended by several additions. A dirt road leads from the street into a large back parking lot. What appears modest on the outside, however, belies what's on the inside: a National Hockey League-sized ice surface, groomed by an NHL-acquired Zamboni, skirted by a fully modern, cozily-heated spectator seating area. That's just for starters.

In Canada, hockey is more than a national pastime; it is a national passion. Almost as soon as pioneers raised churches and schools, they began thinking about ice. Curling, skating, and hockey competed for the pioneers' few recreational hours. Children played on frozen ponds, snow-trampled schoolyards, or cold, hard dirt. A branch cut from a tree sufficed for a hockey stick, and a road apple, frozen solid after dropping from the hind end of a horse, was the puck. In schoolrooms, coffee cans filled with sand hurried hard down chalk-marked lanes in mock curling games. Just as soon as a community was established enough to afford it, volunteers came together to raise a proper building for their cold-weather sports.

The arena is often the heart of a small town. Whether it's dubbed the civic centre, recreation complex, community centre, or simply "the rink," it is the one place that reflects cohesion in a community. Age, race, gender, occupation, financial status, religious orientation—none of the distinguishing markers of society are of any consequence there. All who enter do so on an equal footing. It is the place for curling, hockey, ringette, and figure skating. When the ice is out, the arena's uses are endless. Bench shows, trade fairs, indoor rodeos, concerts, dances, public meetings, clinics, school graduations, wedding receptions, anniversaries—just about any event that requires a large, neutral space takes place in the arena. But construction and maintenance costs are huge. Once a community has its ice complex, it is rarely positioned to build a new one. Rather, upgrades on the original hover almost constantly near the top of the community to-do list. Upgrades to the Warner arena came gradually. Showers, dressing rooms, and a new kitchen were added in the 1980s, and in 2001 more renovations were planned.

With the only artificial ice surface for miles around, Warner's complex was already essential to the region. Parents drove children up to an hour and a half to play there. The 2001 renovations would expand the ice surface and replace the battle-scarred sideboards. Ironically, however, the upgrades coincided with dwindling village population and dismal student enrolment projections. It couldn't have been much of a surprise when the school division announced that Warner's beloved K-12 school was on the chopping block. The cut would slice away Grades Seven to Twelve and carry them off to school in the next biggest town. Once again, creative thinking was required to remedy what was considered an unacceptable change. As far as Warner was concerned, the school was the community's heartbeat—and if the heart is removed, the other organs fail. Already the village was struggling. In the face of adverse conditions, farmers and ranchers were packing up and moving on. Local businesses weren't far behind. Twenty per cent of village homes were on the market. With the school reduced to half its former size, full closure seemed imminent. Warner needed to find a way to keep the children it had, and draw in more.

Warner might be small and out of the way, but its residents are very much in tune with what's going on in the rest of the world, and their attention turned to developments in women's hockey, which was gaining recognition and respect and had recently been named a Winter Olympic sport. But girls who wanted to play continued to find themselves on boys' teams, where they were vastly outnumbered and forced to battle stereotypes in a male-dominated environment. Sandra Nelson, an avid school supporter, along with a handful of other community leaders, conjectured that if Warner could bring girls together to play on an all-girls' team, and if a professional coach were hired to develop a quality training program that dovetailed with the regular school curriculum, the result would be attractive to athletes and parents alike. And if the girls were then scouted by colleges, universities, and professional hockey associations, wouldn't that be great for everyone, including Warner? By inviting girls between the ages of thirteen and eighteen to play hockey there, Warner could not only keep its Grades Seven to Twelve in town, but also gain a reputation as a centre for elite girls' hockey. It could generate visibility and revenue. It might even revitalize the town.

The idea took hold, and in March 2002, when the civic centre held its grand reopening after renovations, the plans for the Warner Hockey School had been pitched and approved. The only task that remained was pulling it off.

The timing couldn't have been better. A month earlier, the Canadian women's hockey team won gold at the Olympics in Salt Lake City, putting women's hockey front and centre in the sports media. Post-secondary institutions were adding it to their programs and girls were feeling more empowered to play than ever before. The time was ripe for Warner to make its move.

Still, a great deal of preparation and research was required if they were to make good on their goal of creating one of the best girls' hockey programs in the country, both educationally and athletically. It was agreed that if they wanted to attract the best possible coach, they would have to pay a salary commensurate with professional Western Hockey League rates. The Warner Community Hockey Society was established to coordinate the entire project, and fundraising began.

Here's what a village of just under 400 determined people can do. It had already raised $500,000 towards arena renovations. Now residents were asked to reach into their pockets again. Launching the hockey school would require an estimated $250,000. It was understood that grants would only go so far, and might be difficult to get for such a novel undertaking. Within weeks, the campaign had generated more than $70,000. Support was huge. Individuals, service groups, businesses and national corporations with local interests came on board. Anyone who had anything to offer gave willingly, whether it was time, money, expertise, or necessary equipment. Homes to billet the anticipated twenty-plus girls were arranged. Everything from garage sales to exhibition hockey games were staged to raise money and promote the future school. A target opening date of September 2003 was set. But it was a tough slog, and despite the thousands of dollars and man hours the town poured into the project, by April 2003 spirits were flagging and hope waning.

As often happens, just when things looked bleakest, help arrived. In Warner's case, it came in the form of the Canadian Broadcasting Corporation. Upon hearing of the community's ambitious and far-fetched goal, CBC Television sent a crew to film a segment for *Hockey Day in Canada*. The program caught the attention of Jamie Wood, a New Brunswick native living in New York State. His passion for hockey had led him into coaching, where he'd already received several honours, including recognition in the Hockey Hall of Fame. By happy coincidence, when Jamie saw the piece on Warner he and his wife had been discussing moving back to Canada to start a family. Here was their opportunity. Jamie phoned the Warner School and inquired about the coaching position.

Renewed enthusiasm and determination flooded the village when Jamie was hired as the director of hockey and head coach for the new Warner Hockey School. His move to Warner with his wife in the summer of 2003 galvanized the community. It was full steam ahead.

The school opened on schedule with a full complement of twenty-three registered students. The "Warner Warriors" came from across the country, from Labrador to British

Columbia, and points in between. Warner had its team, its coach, and its program. Most importantly, with almost two dozen new students, it had saved its existing school.

The first season was a resounding success. With students, teachers, parents, billeting families, coaching staff, and virtually the entire community behind the project, Warner would never look back. At the end of its first year, the girls won the ninth annual "April Ice" female hockey tournament in Calgary, defeating teams from across Canada and the United States. They also travelled to Brampton, Ontario to take second place in the biggest female hockey tournament in North America. That same spring, the Alberta Teachers' Association honoured "the over 10,000 hours of hard work, enthusiasm, pride and teamwork" put into the project by presenting the village and the school with the "School/ Community PR Award." On the same day, the government announced a $99,000 grant towards construction of a new athletes' centre.

All the while, ninety-eight-year-old Rome Meisser had quietly been watching the hockey program's progress. Rome had lived in Warner since he was five. He'd been one of the first to attend the new consolidated school in 1914; he'd been through the fire of 1917 that destroyed the theatre and twenty-seven buildings; he'd watched crops succumb to grasshoppers and drought, grain prices plummet, and village population dwindle to fewer than half its former numbers. He'd seen it all. He was as much a part of Warner as anyone, but had never married. The village was Rome's family, and he believed that families should help each other.

A dormitory that could house up to forty-eight girls had always been part of the plan, but as Rome observed, other priorities consistently ate up available resources. And so, he announced a personal donation of $210,000 to help fund construction of the dorm. The gift was so magnanimous that it made news headlines throughout the region. It's likely that Rome, a loner who'd simply wanted to do something for his town, was disconcerted by all the attention. It's just as likely he was pleased that it spotlighted even more the efforts and success of his tiny village.

The town found the perfect location for the dormitory on the south edge of town, just three blocks from the school and civic centre: a vacant church overlooking a pretty prairie landscape. After discussion with church leaders in the United States, the building was saved from demolition. Once again, children and seniors and everyone in between came together to work side by side, fixing, renovating, sewing, and painting. More fundraisers and more donations furnished and equipped the residence. The finished building contains more than bedrooms; the amenities include a gymnasium-style recreation room, study areas, a television and games room, a kitchenette for between-meal snacking, a dining hall, a laundry, and a self-contained suite for a live-in manager. Rome did not live to witness the grand opening of the Rome Meisser Centre in August 2005, but he did have the satisfaction of knowing the lasting difference he'd made. Each year, girls from places as diverse as Sweden, Texas, and the Rocky Mountains come together in the dorm to live and bond as teammates. Rome will not be forgotten: the Warner

Warriors wear a patch on their uniforms honouring the man who gave them a home away from home.

The extent to which Warner supports its school and its players is exemplified by the actions of the first dorm mother, who not only fed and nurtured the girls, but also donated a portion of her salary back to the program.

The Warner Hockey School gets better and better. After laying a solid foundation, Jamie Wood left in 2007 to coach women's hockey at the university level, and former NHL star Mikko Makela arrived to take his place. He was pleasantly surprised by the skills of the girls. Indeed, they held such an unfair advantage over the other teams that they gave up playing in the Alberta girls' midget hockey league and entered the more challenging Junior Women's Hockey League. The move entailed travelling greater distances to face off against bigger, older players across Canada and the United States, some of whom compete at the international level. As usual, everyone involved rose to the challenge— including the local man who drives the team bus, who soon found himself navigating strange roadways in metropolises like Montreal and Boston. Despite their disadvantage, in two years the girls attained top standing in the new league while maintaining above-average grades. Scouts from universities and colleges such as Princeton, Harvard, Cornell, and Dartmouth routinely cast their eyes towards Warner. Scholarships to grads they've recruited now tally several million dollars. The women's division of Hockey Canada has sent its head scout to run practices there, and the school has produced more than one Olympic hopeful.

Warner's success hasn't come easily. Pockets only reach so deep, and grants have been hard to come by. The state-of-the-art athletes' centre, originally planned for the summer of 2004, wasn't completed until the spring of 2008, but it added a well-equipped training facility and four more dressing rooms, all with showers and washrooms. Like everything about the complex, these additions are for public use, especially for minor hockey—but the presence of the Warriors justifies the superior amenities and equipment. One of the dressing rooms is beautifully appointed in Warner Warriors colours and is dedicated to the elite girls' hockey team. And even though Warner tried and failed two years in a row to win CBC Television's *Kraft Hockeyville*, the annual nationwide quest to find "Canada's most passionate hockey community" and present it with a $50,000 purse for arena upgrades, the effort brought the hockey school a great deal more exposure.

There has been some grumbling within the community, mostly to do with the attention and resources the girls receive to the perceived detriment of the children who play minor hockey, but these rumbles stay well below the radar. It's simply too clear to everyone—even those with complaints—that the benefits of the town's decision outweigh any disadvantages.

The community's efforts to establish the hockey school have clearly been successful. The next challenge is to make the program self-sustaining. To that end, Warner Hockey School is seeking to double enrolment and create two teams. There's little doubt they can achieve this goal.

Nevertheless, Warner is not putting all its eggs in one basket. It is still an agricultural community. Across the country, wooden grain elevators have gone the way of the dinosaur, but Warner has managed to hang onto six which stand side by side along the railroad tracks. This makes Warner home to one of the last two surviving elevator rows in Canada. Inglis, Manitoba, location of the other "last elevator row" has recognized the historical significance of this distinction and is using it to revitalize its town, as described in the next chapter. While Warner has yet to save its elevators from destruction the way Inglis has, it is uniquely positioned to develop and promote the row as an educational and tourist attraction.

And then there is the flight school. Warner School might focus on female hockey players, but its regular students and program are just as important. After all, preventing local students from being bused out of town was why the hockey school was developed in the first place. Most high schools have international student programs, and Warner is no exception. If there was a way to make its student exchange program particularly appealing, Warner could be counted on to find it. The village has an airport, which, like everything else in this small town, is just a short distance from the school. It's a small airport with one runway and two hangars. It's not meant for commercial use, but it's perfect for a flight training school. Now, in addition to learning about western Canadian culture while improving their English skills, international students can leave at the end of the year with more than 100 hours of flight instruction (most of them in the cockpit of an airplane high above the earth) and an internationally recognized private pilot's license.

As long as there are imaginative possibilities to ponder and industrious people to pursue them, the village of Warner won't die. Thanks to their parents' efforts on behalf of the school, children who are fortunate enough to grow up there will inherit a legacy of teamwork, open-mindedness, and a fierce determination to succeed. They are all the Warriors of Warner.

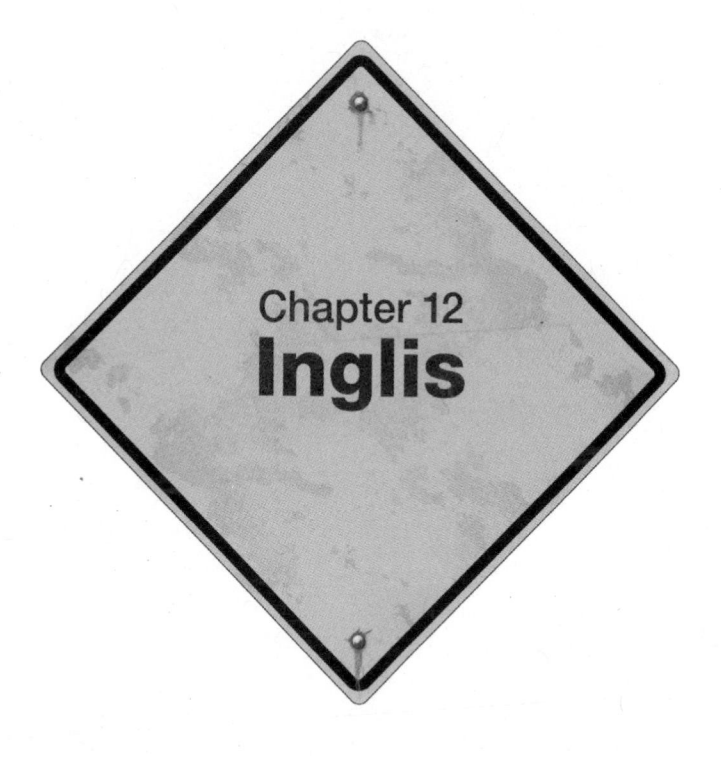

Chapter 12
Inglis

Inglis

Saving the Sentinels

Some might think of Inglis, Manitoba as a falling star, bursting upon the scene in a brief, spectacular dazzle of glory, and then fizzling. Before 1922, the community, 350 kilometres northwest of Winnipeg, didn't even exist; seventy-three years later, it was dying.

But Inglis is no falling star.

Whenever I hear about a town that has defied death, one of the first things I do is look up its population. Then I try to figure out how it managed to beat the survival odds. With Inglis, I did the opposite. After grasping the sheer scale of this community's remarkable achievement, I was stunned to discover that for years, the population had hovered around a mere 200, in a municipality of fewer than 1,000.

Inglis originated in 1922, when the Canadian Pacific

Railway (CPR) extended its line to the spot where the village now stands. In those years, many rail lines (and communities) were built to service the grain industry, and the grain industry certainly served them too. Coincidentally, the community's name was a nod to this stitching together of farming community and railroad; Robert Inglis was the tailor who suited and uniformed CPR executives and railwaymen.

New construction and moved-in buildings rapidly wove together a community. Within a year, four grain companies built elevators. The soil in the region was so rich and fertile and the farmers so keen that in due course Inglis earned the title "Barley Capital of Canada." Six months after the rail line opened, the CPR added passenger transport to freight hauling services. Three days a week, at 7:25 in the evening, the train rolled in from Winnipeg. Inglis shopkeepers made a point of staying open late for any needs the travellers might have. Soon, ease of travel encouraged further settlement, and the future looked bright.

But dark times loomed. The onset of the Great Depression only eight years later put the brakes on growth. It is perhaps here that the extraordinary pluck of community residents first became apparent. They snubbed their collective nose at hardship. A lively social scene defied despair and reinforced the town's continuing energy, optimism, and cohesion. Rather than disband, the local orchestra changed its name to The Gloom Chasers, and kept right on playing. Any excuse for frolic was seized with relish. Dances, plays, debates, card parties, ice sports, and every kind of ball (broom, foot, fast, soft) did chase the gloom away. This attitude towards adversity became ingrained as a trait that made its way down through the generations.

Economically, things didn't pick up again until after the Second World War, when, among other things, a movie theatre was built, electricity arrived, and the need for more storage resulted in the addition of annexes to three of the four grain elevators. Ironically, the last of these was built in the same year the rail line made its first troubling cutback. In 1953, even as the thriving town moved forward with new construction, passenger train service was discontinued, and the worried whispers began. Three years later, amid swirling rumours of imminent rail line closure, Inglis was officially named a village. Here again was irony. Just as the newly incorporated community was starting to grow, it was starting to die.

The loss of passenger rail service seems to have sounded a silent signal. Even though trains still came in to carry grain away, elevator companies became increasingly reluctant to put money and labour into building maintenance. No longer spruced up with fresh paint or diligently repaired, the towering storehouses soon showed signs of neglect. In the 1960s, smaller branch lines across the country began to close, leaving the elevators along them to fall into disuse. They were moved, dismantled, destroyed, or simply abandoned. The main issue was money. In 1995, for instance, Canada's National Transportation Agency recommended the closure of 535 miles of track and thirty-five elevators in Saskatchewan and Manitoba, saving an estimated $14 million in grain transporation. It took years for the country to realize what was happening to its beloved grain elevators—potent symbols of prairie life and prosperity. It's fair to say prairie people didn't recognize how iconic the elevators were until they started disappearing, by which point the crushing wheels of progress had gathered too much momentum to stop.

Concurrent with track closures were grain company amalgamations and buyouts, all in the name of centralization and corporate growth. During their years of use, one pair of elevators in Inglis went through five company name changes. Another elevator—the National—was purchased by Cargill, only to be handed on to N.M. Paterson & Sons a short time later. Neither Cargill nor Paterson bothered to publicly demonstrate its ownership by putting its company colours or name on the building, so the original white "National" logo against a brown background remained. Farmers and elevator agents no doubt grumbled about the changes—little realizing that the grain companies' neglect of Inglis' elevators would one day help save the town.

The age of the railway—the reason for Inglis' being—was coming to a close. Like fine dust, a general unease settled over the area. It took eighteen years from the time passenger service ceased and the rumours began, but in 1971, freight service ended too. By now residents were certain it would be just a matter of time before the tracks were torn out.

They were right. The demise was drawn out, like slow torture, but in 1995, grain shipping by rail ended, and in 1996 the line was abandoned. The last of the working elevators closed for good. Everywhere—at kitchen tables, shop counters and in the streets—the question was the same: would the village die? With its fate inextricably linked to the rails, it looked like the community would come to a premature end just seventy-three years after it was founded.

But the people of Inglis and district had plenty of time to consider their fate. Once again they rallied. Diversification was the key. The focus of the area had always been agricultural—and still is. Today, a U-pick strawberry farm, a prairie plant nursery, equine ranches, and cattle, elk and buffalo farms complement grain farming. Thanks to its location in Manitoba's parkland, the area has other attributes as well. Asessippi Provincial Park, at the convergence of three beautiful valleys, is just minutes away. There, along the shores of the Lake of the Prairies, camping, swimming, hunting, fishing, and a variety of summer activities have been developed. Proliferations of trails etched against the steep slopes lend themselves perfectly to summer hiking and winter skiing.

Resourcefulness and foresight have resulted in the development of Asessippi Ski Area and Winter Park, a state-of-the-art facility that was named "Canada's Best New Attraction" by Attractions Canada in 2000. With more than 100 employees, Asessippi Provincial Park is the largest employer in the area. Tourists come in droves, attracted by the year-round activities, and after an invigorating day of snowboarding, tubing, ice fishing, snowmobiling, and downhill and cross-country skiing, they crave a hot meal and a place to lay their heads.

The park sparked cottage development. In Inglis and the surrounding area, bed and breakfast operations opened, and other spinoff businesses took hold as well.

Village and municipal residents were quite happy to embrace and encourage a resort atmosphere, but their agricultural roots run deep, and when the rail line was abandoned, those who had made their living from the soil were not prepared to sever the ties.

Across the prairies hundreds of communities were in similar straits. For years they had taken for granted the elevators that greeted them a thousand times a day from their windows, stood silently on their way to school, or marked the next town on their travels. The simple structures were plain and familiar—until they began disappearing. When people realized what was happening, a phenomenon occurred. Suddenly, like nostalgic lovers, they began attaching sentimental names to the objects of their affection: prairie giants, prairie sentinels, prairie skyscrapers, wheat kings, gold vaults of the prairies, cathedrals of the prairie. Individuals and entire communities rose up fighting to save their elevators. Some succeeded; most did not. The disappearance of wooden grain elevators took place stealthily, especially as grain companies became aware of the unwelcome uproar that so often resulted. A community's grain elevator might be there one day and gone the next. Often residents wouldn't even know it was scheduled for demolition. Grain companies were reluctant to leave abandoned elevators standing. They were fire hazards and dangerous magnets for children. Taxes had to continue being paid on them. If another company bought the elevators, it posed the threat of competition. Occasionally they were sold to a farmer who took them for grain storage, but often they had to be moved. And when elevators disappeared, the loss of tax revenue alone was often enough to cripple or destroy a small town.

Several months before Inglis' last working elevator was scheduled to close, a group of citizens began to organize. It wasn't merely the prospect of losing the farmers' daily social gathering spot that troubled them; they were keenly aware of what losing five elevators would do to both Inglis' skyline and its bottom line and set themselves an ambitious—some would say outrageous—goal. Much larger towns had struggled and failed to save even one elevator. It was anybody's guess what made a municipality of 875 people believe it could save an entire elevator row.

The Inglis Area Heritage Committee (IAHC) formed in November 1994 to restore the elevator row to its original condition so it could serve as a monument to vanishing prairie culture and architecture. The two companies that by now owned all of Inglis' elevators—N.M. Paterson & Sons and United Grain Growers—gave the committee one year to come up with both a plan and the money to implement it. Otherwise the elevators would be destroyed. If ever there was a time for people to pull together, this was it. Resolve was firm and action swift. By April 1995, the IAHC was incorporated, and in 1996 it succeeded in having the Inglis grain elevators, one of only two elevator rows left in Canada, declared a National Historic Site. This secured the buildings, adding legitimacy to the cause. Support came pouring in.

Working in the project's favour was the fact that the elevators were true originals. Four had been constructed in the early 1920s, when the railway first came to Inglis. The fifth was erected in 1941. It was clear now that the general neglect the elevators had suffered since the 1950s was a blessing. Much of the original architecture and equipment had not been changed or updated. Nevertheless, hundreds of thousands of dollars were required to make the structures safe and restore them completely. It would cost $70,000 alone to re-side one elevator, never mind repairing and refurbishing equipment, replacing shingles, and doing the necessary painting and cleaning on all five. For an area with a population so sparse to raise such money and then somehow do the work was nearly impossible. Rather than let this get them down, however, the committee got to business.

To begin with, they decided to restore one elevator to run as an operating museum and simply stabilize the other four. They worked as the money came in, recycling materials where they could and using local contractors and volunteer labour to save on costs. The elevators' new status as a National Historic Site helped qualify the restoration project for municipal, provincial, and federal grants. Support increased as people witnessed how seriously committed the IAHC was. Many purchased Heritage Committee memberships. Donations ranged from gifts of a few dollars, perhaps given in memory of a loved one, to anonymous bequests of a few thousand, not to mention money raised by local businesses, family foundations, and elevator companies, and ham and turkey bingos, concerts, and lunchtime barbecues. A book, *Backtracking*, was produced and sold, serving to both advertise the site and generate funds.

The committee engaged a communications company to develop a website and media package. Soon Inglis was splashed all over the radio, television, magazines and newspapers. Brochures and posters were distributed, and Travel Manitoba actively promoted the site. A British film crew even arrived to shoot a segment about the unique facility.

When the project reached the point where tours could be offered and a gift shop opened, further revenue streams appeared. It took seven years of work and $2 million raised over more than ten years, but by August 2006 all five elevators—the entire row—had been restored.

Today, visitors to the Inglis Elevators National Historic Site number in the thousands each year. They come to learn about prairie agriculture and architecture. Or they come simply to take a walk down memory lane. (The actual lane is the old rail bed, now the Crocus section of the Trans Canada Trail.) They come from as far away as South Africa, Germany, Holland, Japan, France, England, Australia, Ireland, and Denmark. Some are retired grain buyers; others don't know what wheat is. Schoolchildren come to gain hands-on interactive knowledge of history and the grain industry; bus tours come to see one of Manitoba's most successful restoration sites. Seven days a week from June through August, and during the rest of the year by appointment, students and volunteers conduct tours through the elevators and down the row. Self-guided walking tours are also available, allowing visitors to experience the sights, sounds, smells, tastes, and feel of the prairie.

Local support is astounding. Residents continue to purchase and renew memberships, donate dollars, and offer volunteer hours. The site has become a huge source of pride for the community.

There are other points of pride as well. The Inglis and Area Business Group organized a few years ago to promote the village. They beautified Main Street with benches and planters of flowers, fixed the sidewalks, and commissioned a local artist to paint an impressive mural on the front of the skating rink, showcasing Inglis' core attractions: the elevators, the ski hill, and the Lake of the Prairies. The group arranged for signage directing travellers into the village, billboards for advertising, and Inglis bumper stickers, so residents can trumpet their hometown wherever they go.

Strategies like this are working. Not only are people coming to check Inglis out; some are staying. Newcomers have moved there from as near as Winnipeg and as far away as Vancouver, attracted by the peacefulness and friendly small-town atmosphere as well as the healthy business climate supported by a strong tourist market, cooperative colleagues, and ownership incentives not found in bigger centres.

Now that restoration is complete, the IAHC is working on ensuring that the elevator row will never be threatened again. Fundraising efforts these days are geared towards building an endowment fund of at least $500,000. The principal sum will remain intact while the yearly interest is dedicated to maintaining and sustaining the one-of-a-kind historic site.

Inglis set out to save itself by saving its sentinels. In doing so it saved a prairie culture of the past for a world of present and future generations.

Epilogue

Epilogue

What Does It Take to Save a Town?

Every community is unique and every community has a story. The Willow Bunch giant was an oddity in his Saskatchewan hometown in the late 1800s. But years later his strange life in the circus (and even stranger death) provided a way to spotlight the town. In Torrington, Alberta, a brainstorming session to come up with a way to save the village resulted in the exasperated exclamation that the only thing the town had going for it was its gopher population. A $5,000 government grant, seventy-one stuffed Richardson's ground squirrels, and the backfired outrage of animal rights activists later, the notorious community is still very much on the map. And in Harris, Saskatchewan, a false report of rubies, diamonds, and gold triggered a rush of prospectors to the town in 1914, and for ten wild days, locals charged outrageous prices for basic needs (a dollar for a single egg!), demanded exorbitant fares for rides to the site, pitched a tent over the "ruby rock" (actually a useless lump of stone), charged money just for a peek, and posted an armed guard to ensure the "treasure" wasn't tampered with. (At night, under cover of darkness, the guard sabotaged staked claims nearby and resold them the next day.) The town suppressed any mention of its avaricious behaviour until some brave soul in the mid-1980s boldly stated that the event was part of the town's history and should be told. Today, Ruby Rush Days, a three-day re-enactment of the infamous incident, pokes fun of the town's past and sparks a rush of a different kind each summer.

Most communities have some claim to fame that can be played to advantage. It's a matter of having the imagination, manpower, and often the humour to work with what you've got. But that's not all it takes.

This chapter provides an overview of the characteristics that seem common to towns that revitalize. The list is not exhaustive and should not be viewed as authoritative; it simply outlines patterns that emerged as towns fought against their own demise. The occasional towns cited as examples represent only a few of the many in this book that possess the same attributes. Before summarizing what seems necessary for dying towns to survive, however, it might be useful to note some surprising things that don't seem necessary.

Population: Just look at Lynn Lake (population 714), Big Valley (population 351), and Meacham (population 70). The largest community profiled in this book is Vulcan (population 1,940).

Location: Lynn Lake is a remote northern community; Warner is situated in an out-of-the-way corner of the province. Elbow was pushed off the main thoroughfare when the dam was built and the town lost its bridge. The road to Elbow now is narrow and potholed, yet tourists flock there year-round and new business flourishes.

Basic Services: Schools, post offices, gas stations, and stores are absent from several communities in this book.

Business Opportunities: The Internet, social media, and the global economy mean more and more people have portable livelihoods which they can take almost anywhere. The artists in Meacham, for example, market their wares online as well as in local studios. Business managed from a home office or nondescript commercial building via computer is on the rise. In Herbert, Saskatchewan (population 742), the availability of local work was not even a consideration for several newcomers from Alberta and British Columbia. One runs an Internet-based business from his home and two opened small storefront businesses, supplementing their bottom line with online sales. These people are quick to confirm they moved to Herbert because of the friendly, welcoming atmosphere, personified by the colourful, *Where's Waldo?*-like cartoon character Herbert, who pops up on billboards and buildings to ask out-of-towners "Have you seen Herbert?" or announce, "Herbert has lots for a buck," referring to a new residential development that literally sells "lots" for a "buck." On the highway going past town he entices travellers to "Turn left to see what Herbert has to offer." When they do, they quickly encounter him again on the side of a building, holding a flag of Saskatchewan and saying, "Herbert welcomes you."

Physical Beauty: Empty storefronts, wholly abandoned buildings and vacant lots are still a dominant feature in many of the towns in this book, as are cracked sidewalks (or often no sidewalks at all), gravel streets, and runaway quackgrass. As a side note, these are the very things some find appealing when considering a small town.

With revitalization underway, population, basic services, business opportunities and physical beauty will likely come, but it's clear they aren't necessary to initiate a process of renewal. What does seem necessary, according to the experiences of the towns in this book, are varying combinations and degrees of the following:

Teamwork/Cooperation
• at every level (family, community, regional, provincial, federal)

Open-Mindedness
• acceptance of new and possibly unusual ideas [Craik]
• acceptance of new and possibly unusual people ["Not all of us understand what the artists do," says retired Meacham administrator Betty Saretzsky, "but at least it's population."]
• acceptance of those new and possibly unusual ideas coming from those new and possibly unusual people [Rosebud]

• paying attention to outsiders' perceptions of the town [Vulcan residents took note of the teasing about the size of their ears when the television series *Star Trek* first aired.]

• seriously considering unexpected proposals from outside sources [The street village of Neubergthal wasn't seeking recognition or revitalization when Parks Canada expressed interest in making it a National Historic Site, but residents recognized the potential inherent in the proposition.]

Respect

• for diverse faiths, ethnicities, backgrounds, values; people treating each other as equals [Plum Coulee, Herschel]

Foresight and Hindsight

• ability to recognize advancing decline and devising measures to deal with it before it is too late [Craik, Vulcan]

• ability to either use the events of the past or learn from them [Big Valley, Lynn Lake]

• ability to let go of the past in order to build a future [Lynn Lake]

• willingness to change focus, (e.g. from agriculture to the arts) [Elbow, Meacham, Craik]

Advance Planning

• detailed, focused, preliminary plans outlining both short- and long-term goals. [Plum Coulee and Craik are the best examples of this]

Patience and Perseverance

Volunteerism

• community-wide, spanning all age groups

• donation of time, skills, and goods (in-kind or at cost)

Flexibility

• ability to change course if unexpected circumstances arise [When the creation of Diefenbaker Lake didn't provide Elbow with expected irrigation, it used the reservoir to develop a resort instead.]

• recognizing and seizing opportunities that come to light

Creative Thinking/Imagination

• consideration of every idea, no matter how bizarre or ridiculous it might first seem [Torrington's Gopher Hole Museum, Vulcan's *Star Trek* theme]

• willingness to take risks [see above!]

Sense of Humour

• the ability to laugh at oneself [Big Valley, Harris, Vulcan, Torrington]

Incentives

• to attract new business and population, and retain that which is already there [Plum Coulee, Craik, Herbert]

• town councils willing to work with business owners on an individual basis [as Elbow did with Wayne Berry and Marjorie McPhee]

Creative Fundraising

• exploring every avenue at every level: private donations, corporate and business sponsorship, municipal, provincial, and federal grants [Torrington's grant to stuff several dozen gophers], service club support, fees for services resulting from the project [Craik tours], former residents with means and vested interest [Plum Coulee], book publication [Herschel], fundraising events generating anywhere from a few hundred dollars to a few hundred thousand [Inglis]

Continuing Action

• not stopping once success is achieved and revitalization occurs, combined with a willingness to remain open to further ideas and action [Rosebud, Warner]

Observation/Learning

• studying other communities that have achieved similar goals

• being prepared to learn new things and stretch well beyond the comfort zone [Craik]

Diversity

• emphasizing a specific approach, resource or theme, but not relying on it solely and developing other community strengths as well [Warner's flight training school]

• continuing to support residents and potential residents who aren't interested in the town's new direction [Vulcan still promotes itself as an agricultural community; you don't need to be an environment enthusiast to be welcome in Craik or an arts enthusiast to be welcome in Meacham]

Media Rapport

• recognition that the media can be a true friend—a good story is often shared with affiliated colleagues and spreads like wildfire

• in many cases, even negative media draws positive attention to the town [Paramount turning down Vulcan for a world movie premiere; animal rights activists protesting the stuffing of gophers in Torrington]

Marketing
- creating and keeping current a community website
- making use of other social media (Facebook, YouTube, Twitter, blogs, etc. [Elbow, Vulcan])
- using less high-tech strategies [Inglis bumper stickers; residents of Vulcan wearing their Spock ears or Trekkie costumes away from home]
- creating a town character or mascot [Herbert's "Herbert," Vulcan's "Sehlat"]
- adopting a catchy slogan ["Sail into Elbow," "Have you seen Herbert?"]

Wide Impact
- implementing ideas that benefit more than just the town [Warner advances the careers of female athletes from around the world; Rosebud and Meacham provide platforms for emerging actors nationwide; Inglis and Neubergthal have preserved Canadian prairie history and culture]

Role Models
- key players in community revitalization efforts often act as role models for the rest of the community [The Town of Craik retrofitted town buildings to demonstrate environmental stewardship and affirm its commitment to the new direction]; as more people come on board, even the dissenters are won over

Sustainability
- once a goal is achieved, putting measures in place to maintain it [Warner's plan for expansion, Plum Coulee, Inglis' endowment fund]

Hard Work

• after listening to the talk, being willing to walk the walk [Recall the words of LaVerne Erickson of Rosebud: "Communities are not built by consultants... they are built by committed, hardworking citizens."]

Finally, the ability to accept the changing face of the community is a key component to successful revitalization. Communities pursuing renewal typically don't try to cling to the traditions of the past. When new population is attracted because of what's happening in the town, longtime residents welcome them rather than resent them as intruders. Often those newcomers bring fresh ideas, energy, and commitment, and inspire renewed excitement in the project. They provide relief and respite for those who've been working hard from the beginning and run the risk of burning out. In many small rural communities, a high percentage of the population are either seniors or approaching retirement age. But those who are interested in moving there because they like what the town is doing, or because they're attracted by low taxes and cheaper real estate prices, are often young professionals with families they want to raise in a small-town environment. They typically support community events and get involved in local organizations—coaching sports teams, volunteering on the fire department, or sitting on the school board. When they are financially successful, they put their money back into the community. It's a winning situation for everyone concerned.

Towns that demonstrate the above attributes and

attitudes are models for the children who grow up there. When those children become adults, many will choose to stay in a positive, progressive town. Those who leave will carry the skills and values they've learned to the communities in which they eventually make their lives. Wherever they choose to settle, they will perpetuate the cycle of success.

A final note: this book is not intended as a definitive guide to revitalization. As I say in the prologue, I make no pretense of authority or expertise. I simply set out to tell the stories of twelve towns that are surviving, often against long odds. In addition to satisfying interest and supplying information, it's my hope that *Herbert Has Lots For A Buck* will inspire optimism, courage, creativity, and perhaps the recognition of traits unique to one special place—a town that you know.

Acknowledgements

In homes and in coffee shops, in village offices and in post offices, on street corners and on the Internet I conversed with people about their communities. I am indebted to them for the time they gave me and the open-hearted enthusiasm with which they embraced the subject. Many of those lovely and deserving towns didn't make it into this book, but I will always remember the warm reception they gave me.

Heartfelt thanks to the board of directors of NeWest Press, whose faith in the project never flagged, even when its author did. Dr. Don Kerr's steadfast interest, advice, and support brought me to the finish line. I was honoured to work with Paul Matwychuk, who not only oversaw the publication process, but also delighted me with his meticulous copyediting skills. Many thanks to Greg Vickers for the cover and interior design, and to Andrew Wilmot, Matt Bowes, Tiiu Vuorensola, and the team at NeWest Press for their efforts on behalf of *Herbert Has Lots For A Buck.*

Robert Vogt, Deborah Rea, Wendy Robison, and Darcy Novakowski provided extraordinary support from the beginning. Drs. Roger Epp, Joanne Jaffe, and Debra Davidson gave willingly of their expertise. Thanks to the Claresholm Public Library (Kathy Davies and Karen Uhl) and to the Coaldale and District Chamber of Commerce for leave to research and write. Residencies at the Wallace Stegner House in Eastend, Saskatchewan and with the Shortgrass Library System, in conjunction with the Writers Guild of Alberta, provided the time and the space. A word of acknowledgment must also go to the dauntless librarians of Alberta's excellent Ask a Question (AAQ) service.

Finally, I am profoundly grateful to the Alberta Foundation for the Arts, whose assistance allowed me to complete *Herbert Has Lots For A Buck.*

Elizabeth McLachlan was born in Coaldale, Alberta, and feels fortunate to have lived in eleven rural communities throughout the province. She currently resides in Lethbridge, where she works as a freelance writer, editor, and public speaker. Elizabeth has previously published three books with NeWest Press: *With Unshakeable Persistence: Rural Teachers of the Depression Era*; *With Unfailing Dedication: Rural Teachers in the War Years*; and *Gone But Not Forgotten: Tales of the Disappearing Grain Elevators*.